Workers Who Drink

Workers Who Drink

Their Treatment in an Industrial Setting

Carl J. Schramm
Wallace Mandell
Janet Archer
The Johns Hopkins University

Lexington Books
D.C. Heath and Company
Lexington, Massachusetts
Toronto

Library of Congress Cataloging in Publication Data

Schramm, Carl J.
   Workers who drink.

   Bibliography: p.
   1. Alcoholism and employment—Case studies. 2. Alcoholism—Treatment—United States—Case studies. I. Mandell, Wallace, joint author. II. Archer, Janet, 1947-   joint author. III. Title.
HF5549.5.A4S36   362.2'92'0973   76-58248
ISBN O-669-01342-0

Second printing, February 1980

Published simultaneously in Canada

Printed in the United States of America

International Standard Book Number: 0-669-01342-0

Library of Congress Catalog Card Number: 76-58248

Contents

List of Figures

List of Tables

Preface

This volume reports the results of a demonstration and research project under-
taken to explore a new concept in the organization of alcoholism treatment services and to develop basic data on the labor force behavior of alcoholic workers.

For the demonstration component of the project, twelve private and government service employers, with a combined work force of over 134,000, participated by referring alcoholic employees to a treatment facility especially created
for this study. Also participating in the project were fourteen local unions,
representing the workers of the participating employers. By its very nature,
this combination of union and management interest and cooperation in affecting referrals to a treatment program set up exclusively to handle working alcoholics, marked the Employee Health Program (EHP) as a unique experiment
in organizing alcoholism treatment. As the culmination of a research study
into the characteristics of employed alcoholics, the project provides the most
comprehensive data on an industrial population of alcoholic workers yet to
be compiled.

A brief summary of the organization of this book may help the reader to
distinguish the demonstration and research components of the study. Chapter 1
describes the evolution of the EHP concept, and outlines the major research
and demonstration goals of the project. Chapters 2-4 report on various aspects
of the two-year demonstration project. Chapter 2 presents the organizational
history of EHP from its opening in the summer of 1973 to its closing in the
Fall of 1976, one year after the study period. Chapter 3, which is concerned
with issues in the identification and referral process, details the project's experiences in promoting cooperation among participating companies and unions, and
in evolving the mechanisms for moving patients into treatment. Issues and
assumptions underlying the treatment process are the subject of chapter 4.
Chapters 5-7 summarize the research findings of the project. Chapter 5 is a
detailed description of the study population; chapter 6 compares and contrasts
the social stability, work experiences, and job and life satisfaction of the study
population with that of a group of nonproblem-drinking workers in the same
work force; and chapter 7 discusses the experiences of EHP workers following
treatment. Finally, chapter 8 reviews the EHP experience and outlines the
implications of the project's findings for future research and policy in the area
of industrial alcoholism.

A note about terminology. There is much controversy surrounding the
meaning of the terms alcoholic and alcoholism, and many investigators prefer
the use of other terms, such as problem drinker (or deviant drinker) which do
not imply the progressive loss of control suggested by the word alcoholism.
Because EHP was an *alcoholism* clinic and yet we recognize that the problem

we are studying is a multidimensional one, we use both terms—alcoholic and problem drinker—in this book. But our operating definition is a behavioral one; that is, any worker whose repeated misuse of alcoholic beverages sharply reduces his effectiveness in performing his work responsibilities is an alcoholic or problem drinker.

Acknowledgments

The research reported in this volume has drawn upon the support of many individuals in the Baltimore community. We are grateful to the personnel of the Baltimore Area Council on Alcoholism and to the industrial and government managers who cooperated with us. Likewise, the leadership of the labor unions who participated in the project has been a resource without which our progress would have been impossible. To the representatives of participating managements and unions who gave of their time through participation on the project's advisory board, and whose guidance and counsel have made the tasks of project management easier, we are most appreciative.

The support of the Office of Research and Development of the Employment and Training Administration of the U.S. Department of Labor, and of Mr. Ron Jones in particular, is acknowledged. Finally, the authors are also extremely grateful to the dedicated employees who served both the clinic and research efforts of the project. The particular devotion of Barbara Winkler and Klementyna Dawson to the successful outcome of the project is warmly acknowledged.

Workers Who Drink

Background, Goals, and Scope of the Study

Although definitions of alcoholism vary among researchers and clinicians, there is virtually unanimous agreement that problems related to the misuse of alcohol are a source of concern to our society. It has been estimated that 9 million American men and women are alcohol abusers or alcoholics. An estimated 5 percent of the U.S. work force are alcoholic individuals, and almost another 5 percent are serious alcohol abusers (U.S. Department of Health, Education and Welfare 1971). The legitimacy of examining the importance of alcoholism as a disability affecting work-force behavior cannot be questioned. It has been estimated that each year over $9 billion is lost to the economy from alcohol-related reductions in productivity alone (U.S. Department of Health, Education and Welfare 1974).

Treatment of Alcoholic Workers in Their Employment Setting

Given that the major burden of the costs of this lost productivity is borne directly by the employer, programs to assist alcoholic workers have existed since 1944. During the postwar years, a few pioneering companies sought to identify the alcoholic employee and refer him to treatment. Although no more than 100 companies had established or planned to establish alcoholism programs by 1960 (Winter 1970), by this time companies with active programs were beginning to report treatment success unparalleled in more traditional forms of treatment. Beyond the promise of high success rates, the concept of industrial programs was enthusiastically supported by the alcoholism treatment community, since it was seen as providing a unique possibility for early intervention into the problem-drinking cycle. While conventional forms of treatment had to wait for the alcoholic to come to them (usually only after the problem had progressed to the late stages), it was reasoned that company programs could identify early-stage alcoholics through observing deterioration in work performance. Moreover, the work place offered a preexisting structure for identification and referral in the form of the supervisory process.

Largely through the efforts of private agencies such as the National Council on Alcoholism and the Christopher D. Smithers Foundation, the number of employee alcoholism programs increased between threefold and tenfold from 1960 to 1970 (National Institute on Alcohol Abuse and Alcoholism 1972). Despite this increase, the number of companies with policies or programs

1

represented only a small fraction of U.S. employers. By 1974, however, 34 percent of major private companies in the United States had adopted some form of program to help problem-drinking workers (U.S. Department of Health, Education and Welfare 1974).

The major impetus behind this recent growth in company programs was the emergence of the federal government into the arena of alcoholism treatment and research. Stimulated by members of the alcoholism movement and as an outgrowth of concern in the late sixties over the problem posed by drug addiction, in 1969 Congress passed Public Law 91–616 (the Hughes Act) which created in 1970 the National Institute on Alcohol Abuse and Alcoholism (NIAAA) to guide national efforts in attacking alcohol problems. Among the branches within NIAAA designed to deal with alcohol problems of special populations was the Occupational Programs Branch whose target population was employed problem drinkers. The Occupational Programs Branch provided funding for company-based treatment efforts in primarily two forms: grants to provide consultation at the local level to encourage and assist companies in launching treatment programs, and funding for demonstration projects to explore alternative models and methods of reaching and treating employed problem drinkers.

In addition to the efforts of the NIAAA to bring into focus the relevancy of the place of employment as an opportunity to initiate early treatment, the U.S. Department of Labor also became interested in the problem of alcoholism and its effects on the work force. Nevertheless, in a 1970 article on industrial alcoholism in the Department's magazine *Manpower*, it was concluded that the current state of knowledge and research on the problem did not provide an adequate basis for establishing public policy and programs regarding drinking and the labor force. Indeed, despite the proliferation of the company treatment concept and its implementation nationwide, basic research into the job-related components of alcohol misuse and the work behavior of problem drinkers occupies only a small space within the growing literature on industrial alcoholism.

Employee Health Program

Reflecting the concerns of both, in 1972 the U.S. Department of Labor and NIAAA joined forces to award a three-year grant to the School of Hygiene and Public Health of the Johns Hopkins University to study the problem of "retaining problem drinkers on the job." Shortly after funding was approved and the operational planning had begun, the project became known as the Employee Health Program (EHP).

The negotiations which gave rise to the EHP project began in 1970 between the Johns Hopkins research group and the Department of Labor. After considering a number of possible methods of gathering data on a population of problem-drinking workers, it was decided that actual workers should be studied so that comprehensive information on work history not available through secondary data sources could be compiled. To assemble a population of alcoholic workers of sufficient size for the research goals of the project, a single-situs treatment facility was envisioned to which several Baltimore companies and unions would refer problem-drinking workers for treatment.

The decision to operate a clinic was made for reasons beyond the goals of research, however. Baltimore—like several other American cities, including Boston and Milwaukee— has had a long-standing tradition of special alcoholism treatment efforts. As part of this community interest, some attention had already been paid to alcoholics in their work roles. Several Baltimore companies had more-or-less active treatment programs, and a number of unions had part-time personnel assigned to alcoholism counseling. Moreover, the need for formalized treatment for alcoholic workers had been strongly promoted by the Metropolitan Council of AFL-CIO Unions as early as 1964, when a two-day conference on the subject was convened in the state capital. Additionally, in assembling a population of individual workers who had been identified as alcoholics, it was recognized that a means for treating them would be imperative. The scandal of Public Health Service-sponsored research which allowed known carriers of syphilis to continue untreated so that later stages of the disease could be observed, emphasized the need to offer a treatment regimen to identified alcoholics. Moreover, union leadership was concerned over the risk of job loss that would accompany identification of alcoholic workers.

As a consequence, it was decided to operate the treatment facility as a demonstration project of a clinic providing services to identified workers to protect them from the risks of job loss, and as an experiment to test the concept of the consortium treatment approach. Because of NIAAA's involvement in the funding of demonstration alcoholism clinics, the Department of Labor invited NIAAA to review the proposal. The resulting EHP grant involved cosponsorship with the Department of Health, Education and Welfare (HEW) funding the clinical arm of the project, and the Department of Labor funding the research, although, as will be seen in chapter 2, the Department of Labor emerged as exclusive funder during the first year of clinic operation.

In June 1973, after months of study and preparation, the Johns Hopkins University opened the Employee Health Program clinic. The name reflects an attempt to mask what was an exclusively outpatient treatment program for employed alcohol abusers in order to reduce public identification and stigma for the referred individuals. Through formal agreement, twelve major employers in the Baltimore Metropolitan area and fourteen local labor unions which represented the employers' work forces, particpated in the project by referring problem drinkers. Although small in number, the firms represented a diversified spectrum of industries and products, from manufacturers of primary steel and automobiles to government service agencies. In all, over 134,000 workers were eligible for the EHP treatment services. In exchange for free clinical services, the employers agreed to supply information on each referred employee to the research staff in order to monitor his progress and job performance.

The research component of the project was located at the Johns Hopkins School of Hygiene and Public Health, under the direction of a research team having expertise in the areas of psychiatry, economics, psychology, and sociology.

Demonstration Goals

As stated above, a major form of federal support for company-based treatment efforts has been the funding of demonstration projects designed to explore the feasibility of alternative models for reaching employed problem drinkers. The basic emphasis of most of these projects had been for the employer or union to assume the major responsibility for the program after the demonstration phase, tying in with local treatment resources. Similarly, a major condition of the grant establishing EHP was that the clinic strive for and achieve self-sufficiency by October 1975, the date of termination of government support. Essentially the consortium, or multiemployer approach, exemplified by EHP was an experiment to test whether a single set of referral, counseling, and treatment services shared by several employers and unions was a workable treatment model. Thus, takeover of the clinic by participating employers or unions after expiration of federal funding would serve as proof of both the need for and the acceptability of the multiparty concept.

The decision to operate EHP as an outpatient facility was seen as one possible obstacle to its prospects for self-sufficiency. At the time of EHP's inception, insurance coverage for outpatient treatment for alcoholism was virtually nonexistent. Therefore, the development of third-party reimbursement for outpatient alcoholism treatment for use by working alcoholics was among the project's demonstration goals.

As will be discussed at length in chapter 3, effecting cooperation between often conflicting union and management interests in alcoholism treatment has presented a problem for company alcoholism programs. Therefore, developing labor-management cooperation within each company on the question of alcoholism among the work force was a major demonstration goal. Additionally, basic to the success of any alcoholism program is the parties' ability to move identified workers into treatment. Again, as discussed in chapter 3, refining and making workable the identification and referral capabilities of participating firms proved to be among the most perplexing and challenging of the project's tasks. Accordingly, through its experiences both in shaping referral mechanisms and in observing their actual operation in a number of different employment settings, the project hoped to contribute to the expanding literature on company identification and referral systems.

Research Goals and Data

Previous research has yielded a small body of basic knowledge on the characteristics of employed problem drinkers as well as many untested suggestions.
It is generally agreed that problem-drinking workers remain in the labor force
while in the early and middle stages of their affliction and that they tend to have
many years of service with their employers. But there is little understanding of
the factors, both sociodemographic and work-related, that may distinguish them
from their nonproblem-drinking counterparts in the work force. Additionally,
a number of recent studies have hypothesized a link between alcohol misuse and
employment-related stresses, such as job content, span of control, and work
environment (O'Toole et al. 1973).

Research Goals

By contrasting the sociodemographic characteristics, work experiences, and job
satisfactions of the EHP study population of employed alcoholics with those of
a comparison group of nonproblem-drinking workers, the research hoped to
develop a more complete understanding of the correlates of problem drinking
among employed individuals.

Another major goal of the research was to determine the efficacy of treatment in prolonging the labor force participation of alcoholic workers. One of
the concerns underlying the Department of Labor's research interests in industrial alcoholism was the possible downward mobility and eventual termination
from the labor force which might occur with progressive alcohol abuse. There-
force, data were compiled on the job retention experiences of study workers
following treatment. The research also hoped to determine whether there were
differences between workers who were terminated and those who were retained
in their jobs after both types had been similarly identified as problem drinkers.

Data

The primary source of data on referred workers was the intake questionnaire, a
copy of which appears in the appendix. The questionnaire, which took a little
over one hour to complete, was administered to each patient at some time
during the first two weeks of his interface with the clinic. The intake questionnaire covered six major areas: circumstances surrounding referral and attitudes
toward treatment, current employment experience and history of labor force
participation, income, attitudes and satisfactions toward the job, personal and
demographic characteristics, and drinking behavior and treatment history. The
questionnaire was administered to 219 patients referred to the clinic between

June 1973 and June 1975. While almost 400 patients were seen during this period, the study population was limited to a size large enough for analysis but small enough to permit continuous tracking of patients for follow-up analysis. Of the patients on whom questionnaire data were obtained, only thirteen were women, partly because the majority of referrals were made by manufacturing companies with predominantly male work forces. Because there were so few women, the study population was restricted to the 206 male referrals. The procedures used to ensure the reliability and validity of the questionnaire are summarized in the appendix.

In addition to the questionnaire data on the study population, data were obtained on a comparison group of nonproblem-drinking workers in order to compare characteristics of referred workers with those of nonalcoholics in the same work force. The comparison group consisted of 100 male workers employed by the twelve referring companies. Because the participating companies were reluctant to supply the project with the names and addresses of their work forces, the comparison group was obtained by using telephone listings from Baltimore area neighborhoods proximate to the locations of referring employers. Using an abbreviated version of the intake questionnaire, telephone interviews were conducted, matching respondents with study workers on age, race, and occupation as well as employer.

The final source of data reported in this volume relates to the job retention experience of EHP workers after they entered treatment and to clinic attendance (i.e., continuation in or withdrawal from treatment). In lieu of the elaborate follow-up data on work performance and drinking behavior that were originally to have been gathered to assess the impact of treatment (as will be discussed in the following section), these data were compiled from clinic records in February 1976 to gain some insights into treatment outcomes.

Limitations of the Data

Several obstacles to data collection occurred that limited the nature and amount of information available to the research component of the project. The major obstacle came in the form of employer noncompliance in supplying requested information, despite promises to do so upon joining the program.

As originally conceived, the research design relied on five separate data sets to be supplied by participating employers. The first two data sets were to be "before" and "after" work histories on each patient sent to the clinic. The "before" work history form which was sent to the employer by the research staff each time a new patient was referred to the clinic requested data on the absenteeism, accident, promotion/demotion, wage, and disciplinary action experience of the worker in the two years prior to referral. Follow-up work history forms, requesting the above information during the year immediately following referral, were sent to the employer twelve months after the worker's first clinic appointment. While 129 work history data forms on work experience prior to referral were returned by employers, the project received complete follow-up data (work history one year after referral) on only thirty patients. The low percentage of employers who supplied follow-up data probably reflects the inability or willingness of employers to devote the resources in staff time required to complete the data forms. The greater compliance demonstrated in completing the original work histories may have become diluted as employers recognized that the chore of supplying personnel data required greater resources than they had anticipated. Moreover, the task of providing data to the project was delegated to personnel department clerks for whom compliance meant added work for a project in which they had little or no involvement or interest.

Employers' failure to supply the other data sets, however, may have been related to second thoughts about the wisdom of releasing potentially "sensitive" information. Thus, no employer submitted problem employee registry forms indicating referrals to other treatment programs (the third data set). The absence of this information seriously limited the ability to judge secondary effects of the project's activities as well as to estimate the degree of penetration achieved. Additionally, firms and agencies refused to provide lists of their work forces (the fourth data set) from which the comparison group could be randomly drawn, fearing the annoyance this might cause among employees contacted for interview. This aspect of noncompliance resulted in the need to rely on telephone listings to assemble the comparison group. Finally, and perhaps also because of the sensitivity of the information, firms declined to supply the project with data on the racial and occupational status positions of the work forces at risk. Without such information, it was not possible to evaluate precisely the extent to which study workers differed from other employees in the work forces from which they were referred.

In addition to employer noncompliance, the data collection effort was hampered by the slow rate of referrals during the first months of clinic operation. The original research design had called for before-treatment and after-treatment assessments of the study population, not only on work-behavior criteria to be supplied by employers, but also on patients' self-reports of changes in drinking behavior and overall life adjustment following treatment (primarily through a repeated application of selected questions on the intake questionnaire). However, in June 1975, when the longitudinal analyses were to have been made, only one-third of the study population had been referred to treatment a year or more earlier, making follow-up impossible at that time.[1] Consequently, the data obtained on outcomes due to treatment were restricted to the criteria of job retention and clinic attendance. These data were compiled from clinic records on February 15, 1976, at which time 85 percent of the study population had been referred to treatment a year or more earlier.

A final problem tending to limit the nature of available data concerns limitations inherent in studying a treatment population of referred alocholic workers. Time-sequence comparisons of behavior before and after a given therapeutic intervention, such as the job retention and clinic attendance of EHP study workers after treatment, cannot take into account many factors which may also contribute to the outcome. To control for such variables would require a true comparison group, that is, workers known to be alcoholics but who did not receive treatment. Even if employers were able and willing to identify such workers and to provide information on their work behavior, such an approach would be precluded by the ethical constraints against allowing identified workers to go untreated for research purposes.

Implications of a Blue-collar Population

With few exceptions, the study populations providing data on the job aspects of problem drinking are composed of workers who have been identified through company alcoholism programs. Large-scale, random samples of problem-drinking workers are difficult and costly to secure, while company-identified problem drinkers constitute readily available, albeit imperfect, research populations. Moreover, since the government and private agencies providing most of the funding for work-centered alcoholism studies have been primarily interested in treatment results, those investigators concerned with developing basic data on the labor force behavior of problem drinkers have had to work with samples of workers that, while not necessarily representative of the problem-drinking labor force as a whole, are often the only ones available for study and evaluation.

Given the nature of the populations available for analysis, that is, company-identified problem drinkers, it is not surprising that much of the emphasis in the research literature on industrial alcoholism has been centered around the mechanisms of company alcoholism identification, referral, and treatment systems. The most notable feature of such systems has been their tendency to produce treatment populations composed primarily of low-status blue-collar workers (Trice 1965a; Warkov et al. 1965), and the EHP population is no exception. Although the program was designed for all problem-drinking workers of participating employers, those referred to EHP were primarily blue-collar workers, with professional and other white-collar workers highly underrepresented (only 20 percent of the treatment population).

Since findings from large-scale samples indicate that neither alcoholism (Straus and Bacon 1951), problem drinking (Cahalan and Room 1974), nor heavy drinking (Cahalan et al 1969) are restricted to any one social or occupational status grouping, it seems likely that the predominance of problem-drinking workers in lower-status occupations in company alcoholism treatment populations is an imperfect reflection of the epidemiology of alcoholism.[2] Alcoholism scholars have observed that social class acts as a selecting factor, both for the identification of alcoholics and for the type of therapies they receive once in treatment (Schmidt et al. 1970). It has been found that the alcoholism of middle-class persons often goes undetected by treatment personnel, while lower-class alcoholics are readily identified as such (Blane et al. 1963). Trice's findings on problem-drinking job behaviors suggest an additional factor that may reinforce this tendency toward differential identification, that is, the nature of the work role itself. Since white-collar middle-class jobs are subject to less supervision, are less interdependent with the work of others, and afford more opportunities for self-cover-up, the problem drinking of such higher-status workers is more likely to go unnoticed than that of blue-collar employees whose job behaviors are more visible to supervision.

The tendency of supervisors in company alcoholism programs to identify and refer workers in predominantly low-status occupations has become a major concern among funders and promoters of such programs, since the uneven distribution of referred workers suggests that many problem drinkers are escaping identification and thus are going untreated. Indeed, those company treatment programs having a predominantly blue-collar makeup are often viewed as failures of the identification and referral mechanism, since it is often assumed that the occurrence of problem drinking "becomes increasingly significant to the company as the position and responsibilities of the employee are greater" (Warkov et al. 1965). This latter attitude betrays a long-standing bias in the emphasis of promoters of industrial alcoholism programs; namely, that employers will adopt treatment programs for their workers only if they are persuaded to do so on the basis of cost-benefit considerations (Roman and Trice 1976). It is not our intention to quarrel with this attitude, but simply to point out that the problems caused by alcohol misuse are no less real and no less a burden to the employer and society when they are experienced by blue-collar workers.

Researchers are only recently coming to recognize that the blue-collar alcoholic has a unique set of problems and that not only the mechanisms for bringing him to treatment, but the nature of his treatment as well, will have to be different from those of more highly skilled, higher-status workers (Trice and Beyer 1977). The question of who *should* bear the costs for identification and treatment—employers, unions, government, or some combination of all three—is a matter of values that need not concern us here. We will, however, present our experiences with one form of identification, referral, and treatment system which we hope will yield some information that may be of use to those who will have to make such value judgments.

Because of the obstacles and limitations to the data outlined in the preceding section, the research data on the social and work characteristics and on treatment outcomes reported in this volume must be viewed as primarily descriptive and exploratory. Nevertheless, these data on the study population are the only detailed set of basic information on the social and work characteristics of blue-collar alcoholics compiled to date. While this population does not allow us to test hypotheses about the nature of alcoholism among workers, it has yielded insights into a number of issues which we hope can serve as a point of departure for future investigators. In particular, the comparison of the EHP study population with a group of their nonproblem-drinking counterparts suggests a need to reexamine a number of our conceptions of the correlates of alcohol misuse by industrial workers.

History of the Program

As an organization faced with the complexities of coordinating the efforts and interests of multiple parties in addition to those inherent in launching a new clinical effort, the Employee Health Program (EHP) offers experiences that encompass a broad range of issues in the field of industrial alcoholism. Following a brief description of the organizational and staffing structure of EHP, this chapter describes, in broad, chronologic form, the problems encountered by EHP in developing a new treatment concept.

Organization and Staff

The organizational structure of EHP is shown in figure 2-2. The day-to-day management and locus of decision making within EHP fell to the project's executive committee. The committee was responsible to the university's central administration, which in turn was the contracting party to the Department of Labor. The executive committee was composed of the principal investigator, the director of clinic treatment (the head counselor), the director of clinic administration (the clinic's business officer), and the director of research. Also joining the executive committee on an irregular basis was the clinic's psychiatrist. The executive committee met weekly to oversee the project's activities.

The purpose of the advisory board, composed of representatives of the participating managements and unions as well as several members of the Baltimore alcoholism community, was to advise the executive committee and to consider policies for stabilizing and continuing the program after the demonstration phase.

In direct-line authority under the executive committee were the Baltimore Area Council on Alcoholism (BACA), the Metropolitan Baltimore Council of AFL-CIO Unions, the clinic staff, and the research personnel. BACA was under contract to the executive committee to develop in-service training programs for personnel in the participating industries and to act as liaison with management representatives of member employers. The Council of AFL-CIO Unions established liaison with participating unions.

Essentially four types of personnel were employed by the project: physicians, counselors, liaison officers, and clerk-secretaries. As of the summer of 1975, three part-time physicians attended the program, with each supplying about four hours per week.

11

12

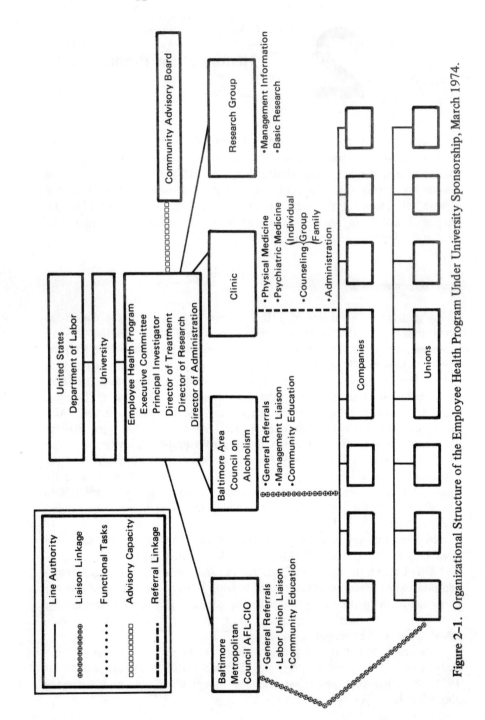

Figure 2–1. Organizational Structure of the Employee Health Program Under University Sponsorship, March 1974.

By far the most important personnel were the counselors. The project attempted to keep the case load of each at or below thirty-five. Because new referrals require extra attention, it was an operating rule that in any one month a counselor would handle no more than five new cases. Given the growing active case load, the clinic grew from two to five counselors by the end of the second year. A number of criteria were used in selecting counselors. First, since black patients formed a large percentage of the case load, it became important to have several black counselors with whom patients could develop a special relationship. While at no time were patients assigned to counselors on the basis of race, the presence of black counselors in the clinic and in conducting group therapy sessions proved reassuring to black patients. A second criterion was to maintain a mix of women and men on the counseling staff. Female counselors proved to be very effective, especially in working with black male patients. Two female counselors worked in the clinic throughout the second year of operation. Finally, the counseling staff always included at least one recovered alcoholic who was a member of Alcoholics Anonymous (AA). The presence of a recovered alcoholic served as a constantly present object lesson to patients that recovery was possible.

Since employers and unions would need both stimulation and support in their efforts to refer alcoholic employees to the clinic, the project appointed liaison personnel to provide educational and training services as well as to oversee the interaction of participating employers and unions with the project. The principal criteria used in selecting liaison personnel were their potential acceptability to participating managements and unions and a thoroughgoing understanding of alcoholism as a problem in the work force.

Secretarial needs were substantial due to the detailed records kept on each patient and the volume of telephone calls and correspondence required to keep track of referred patients. The program employed two secretaries and a receptionist at the close of the second year of clinic operation.

Initiating a New Treatment Facility

Any new health care facility faces two immediate tasks: to gain acceptance by the community as providing an acceptable level of services, and to establish a clientele. Although EHP was identified with a respected medical institution (Johns Hopkins) and had a prearranged clientele, the first year of clinic operation was a struggle to fulfill both tasks.

The Problem of Community Resistance

The project's planners had anticipated that EHP would meet with a certain degree of community resistance as it sought to gain acceptance in a metropolitan area which already had eight outpatient, inpatient, and partway residential programs devoted exclusively to the treatment of alcoholics. Organizational theory suggested that a new program, particularly one which projected a high-level professional image and which established an "exclusive" target catchment population, would be seen as a threat to existing programs and an implied criticism of the level of services that they provided. Finally, the Baltimore alcoholism treatment community has always appeared to be suspicious of treatment efforts not in the tradition of AA. EHP, with its staff of physicians, psychiatrists, counselors, and liaison personnel, was certain to contrast with that tradition.

In anticipation of these problems the preproject planners devised three strategies to minimize community resistance to EHP. The first was to integrate a highly visible part of the established alcoholism community into the project by turning over the labor and management liaison activities to the Baltimore Area Council on Alcoholism. The second was to develop and structure a community advisory board that would have actual decision-making power and that would eventually take an ownership interest in the project. By asking a number of the most visible leaders of the alcoholism establishment to serve on the board, a direct channel would be opened for communicating the project's views on all issues to the persons who ultimately could decide the future of the project, namely, those who controlled referrals. The third strategy was to ensure that the counseling staff of the project always included at least one person who was a member of AA. While having no formal structure, AA provides a common experience of such impact that its members share in a social network of great strength. Establishing the credibility of the program with this network was important because many of the counselors working in other community agencies and programs were former alcoholics who had recovered with the help of AA. Additionally, several participating employers and unions had AA members serving as full-time or part-time alcoholism counselors or had an employee known to be a former alcoholic on whom they could call to help other alcoholic workers.

Despite these attempts to ease the project into the community, resistance began to mount shortly after the program became operational, and persisted throughout the first six months. The resistance took several forms, including the circulation of stories portraying the research interests of the project as involving experimental medical and psychiatric treatment as well as an increased interest shown to EHP employers by other alcoholism programs, reminding them that they could send problem workers to longer-established treatment facilities.

Because of this unanticipated level of resistance, the project began to establish communications with the other treatment facilities and programs in an attempt to dispel their fears and to suggest possible avenues for cooperation. For example, the project worked out arrangements with residential programs to refer EHP patients needing inpatient care to them. Those facilities funded on the basis of patient volume were allowed to count both patients they referred to EHP as well as EHP patients sent to them.

The problem posed by community resistance began to ebb roughly around the sixth month of clinic operations, at which time overtures were made to the program to join the local alcoholism establishment. The authors are convinced, however, that the most important factor in this change of attitude was the low rate of patients referred during the first six months. Thus, only when programs became reassured that EHP did not decrease demand for other services was it welcomed as a member of the existing treatment community.

The Problem of Generating Patient Load

The program was originally funded through a joint mechanism bringing together three years of support from both the National Institute on Alcohol Abuse and Alcoholism (NIAAA) and the U.S. Department of Labor. Since its founding in 1971, NIAAA has shifted between two approaches regarding the proper treatment of industrial alcoholism. The EHP project was conceived and funded during an "exclusively alcoholism phase," but during the summer of 1973, NIAAA policy was rapidly shifting toward broad-brush approaches.[1] Since NIAAA was also faced with budgetary cutbacks, its new priorities, coupled with an internally made estimate of EHP's chance for survival, led to the Institute's withdrawal of support from the project in September 1973. The Department of Labor was then faced with the decision of whether to nearly triple its original funding commitment to ensure the continuation of the project. An evaluation of the clinical operation was begun which soon focused on the poor rate of referrals to the clinic.

Whereas original projections had called for an annual load of 250 patients, there had been only fifty-two referrals to the clinic during the initial six months. In part, the slow rate of referrals was due to factors largely beyond the control of the project, that is, the problem of community resistance and the fact that the clinic had opened in June (July and August are traditionally slow months for referrals in all medical programs). Therefore, the outcome of the Labor Department's evaluation was to continue funding for a six-month trial period to determine whether referrals could be increased to a rate which would produce a large enough population to meet the research goals of the project. To accomplish this, the number of participating employers was expanded from eight to twelve, and other nonmember employers were encouraged to refer workers to EHP on a "trial basis," in the hopes that they would eventually become members. These measures increased the work force at risk of bona fide participating firms from 89,000 to more than 134,000. Additionally, one labor liaison and one management liaison were added to the staff, effectively doubling referral-stimulating capacities. As a result of these steps, the second six months saw an increase of seventy-nine new patients referred to the clinic. Satisfied with the project's ability to generate cases, in March 1974 the Labor Department decided to provide an additional eighteen months of funding.

Reorganization, Consolidation, and Growth

The clinic was able to survive the crisis raised by the slow rate of referrals during the first year of clinic operation, but not without serious disruptions. Since the treatment staff had been developed to handle a growing case load of about twenty new patients a month, staff members were becoming bored and anxious in the face of a seemingly small demand for their services. This, coupled with uncertainty over future funding, prompted staff members to investigate other employment prospects. The net result was that the entire counseling staff had to be replaced in the last months of the first year. Thus, the second year of clinic operation began with a new staff and, as will be seen below, a new administration.

Issues in Clinic Administration

The crisis surrounding the slow rate of patient referrals precipitated a reevaluation of all aspects of clinic operation, one of which concerned administration. Alcoholism treatment programs can be broadly divided into those which operate on a medical model and those which operate on a social service model. Programs following the medical model have a high degree of physician input and operate on the assumption of physical illness; patients enter treatment by referral and are individually diagnosed, treated, and released. In the social service model, the major professional input is from counselors and social workers, entrance is gained through a default process (as in public inebriate programs in which the alcoholic has no other place to go), and treatment consists of adjusting the individual's environment as well as counseling him. Progress through treatment is not always clear, and a discrete discharge point is seldom reached. While EHP had elements of both the medical and social service models, it most clearly resembled the medical model. Treatment was always directed under the supervision of physicians and a disease concept of alcoholism was controlling. EHP patients were referred by a fixed number of employers or unions and the treatment process was viewed as close-ended.

Consistent with its adherence to a medical model, the project employed a physician on a full-time basis to oversee the treatment of patients and the organization of the clinic. This proved to be a very costly deployment of physician hours because there was an actual demand for only ten to fifteen hours of medical care per week, but at least thirty hours were required for administrative chores. Moreover, the status of physicians in a broader societal context makes it particularly difficult to deal with them as employees. At several key points, the executive committee had problems in making the physician-director conform to its policies and procedures. Consequently, at the end of the first year, the physician-director was replaced by a full-time administrator and a counselor-director, and part-time physicians were recruited from among community-based general practitioners and medical residents in nearby hospitals.

Accessibility of Treatment

Another issue that emerged during EHP's period of self-scrutiny was the geographic location of the clinic. Because of concerns for patients' safety, attractive surroundings, and access to the city's high-speed beltway, the clinic was located in a professional building in a suburban neighborhood north of the city. However, after the clinic had been operating for several months, it became apparent that referring persons were reluctant to offer the long trip to the clinic as the only treatment option, and that some workers who were referred dropped out rather than make the trip on a periodic basis. Consequently, a survey of EHP patients' traveling experiences was conducted, and it was found that the bulk of the patient population lived along an east-west axis in the community far from the clinic. The survey also uncovered the fact that many workers felt uneasy over the suburban location itself. To a person who spent the majority of his life in a lower-income, predominantly black neighborhood, the clinic represented a threatening experience.

The staff examined alternative sites closer to the center of the city, and chose a new site that was convenient both to the residences and places of employment of the majority of patients. The decision to relocate was immediately vindicated in both referral and revisit rates. Table 2-1 shows the immediate response in revisits after moving the clinic in early October 1974.

Routinization of the Referral Mechanism

In many respects increase in patient load is the best measure of clinic growth. By the end of the second year the ratio of active cases to referrals, which had been 0.49 at the end of the first twelve months, decreased to 0.32 due to the discharge of patients seen during the first year and the stabilization of new referrals at about twenty per month during the second. Figure 2-2 shows the growth of the ninety-day patient load and the increase in new referrals.

It had been an operating hypothesis of the project's management that once the program was firmly established in the community, new referrals would be made without stimulation. Consequently, during the third six-month period, the project's liaison activity was cut back to one person each in management and labor. As anticipated, both clinic referral and revisit rates continued to

Table 2-1
New Referrals and Clinic Visits by Month

Month	Referrals	Cumulative Total	Clinic Revisits[a]	Cumulative Total
June–1973	3		11	
July	9	12	35	46
August	4	16	42	88
September	8	24	64	152
October	15	39	83	235
November	13	52	92	327
December	11	63	99	426
January–1974	19	82	121	547
February	14	96	136	683
March	12	108	141	824
April	12	120	152	976
May	11	131	137	1113
June	15	146	123[b]	1236
July	15	161	215	1451
August	25	186	301	1752
September	17	203	347	2099
October	18	221	427	2526
November	24	245	363	2889
December	22	267	382	3271
January–1975	15	282	409	3680
February	17	299	331	4011
March	14	313	360	4371
April	17	330	376	4387
May	23	353	429	4816
June	16	369	573	5389
July	22	391	523	5912

[a]Includes all visits less new visits.

[b]This low reflected the inevitable disruption in patient care which occurred as a result of the complete changeover in counseling staff.

increase. In June the management liaison position was cut back to a half-time job, and the labor liaison activity was halted altogether.

Promoting Financial Self-sufficiency

From the outset of the project, one goal dominated all others—the eventual transformation of the clinic from a federally financed and university operated demonstration into a financially independent, community-owned treatment resource.

Funding Options

Three major avenues of future funding for the clinic were under consideration from the time of initial project planning: fee-for-service payment, underwriting by the participating parties, and third-party reimbursement.

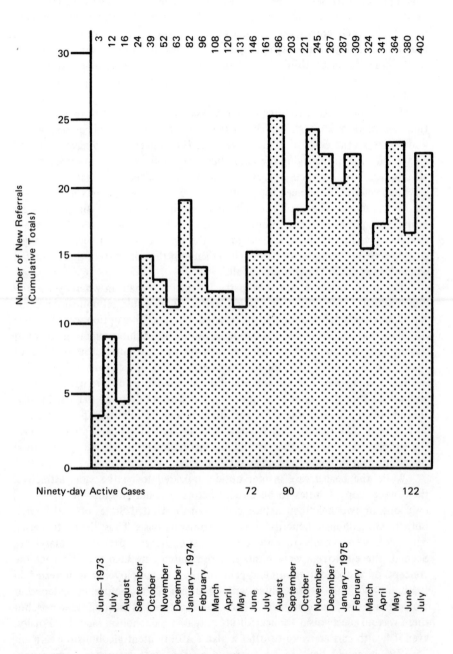

Figure 2-2. Ninety-day Patient Load and New Referrals to the Employee Health Program by Month for the First Twenty-six Months.

The fee-for-service method assumed that patients referred to the clinic would pay cash for services rendered by EHP and be reimbursed by the employer or that employers would send payment directly to the clinic for treatment received by their employees. A disadvantage of the fee-for-service method was that most employers are not equipped to pay health care bills directly because of the role played by third-party carriers. An employer reimbursement scheme would have involved establishing a new set of procedures and policies in the employers' purchasing department.

The second future funding option considered was financing via a subscription mechanism through which participating employers and unions would underwrite all the costs of clinic operations. This concept would have permitted greater latitude in managing the clinic than the fee-for-service option since with all costs underwritten, clinic growth could be controlled by actual demand for services rather than the need to maintain large patient loads to maximize fee-for-service revenues. The problems associated with this type of financing were primarily equity concerns among the parties. Whereas some employers might have been willing to make a fixed gift to the project, others argued for a cost-sharing scheme, prorated to the employer's use of the clinic; still others doubted whether they could "contribute" at all.

The third option was a third-party payment mechanism whereby the employer's health care insurer or a union welfare fund would reimburse the clinic for all services actually rendered to referred workers. This option was attractive for many reasons. Foremost was that since third-party reimbursement is the most widely accepted and understood means of health care policy, the problem of finding an acceptable or common third-party payer never arose. Additionally, insurance companies had already established a modality for arranging payment and would provide a system of uniform rates acceptable to all parties. Finally, the employer's contribution for the clinic would be relatively painless under such a plan. The health carrier would add an across-the-board premium onto the employers' policies that would be inconsequential relative to the total premiums paid for all health and surgical coverage.

While the health care insurer option appeared to be the most attractive, there were many hurdles to be crossed before it could be implemented. First, only one or two health insurance carriers in the United States offered limited outpatient alcoholism benefits on an experimental basis. Thus, the participating employers were unable to purchase an existing benefit package in Maryland. Second, the employers were hesitant about purchasing such benefits since the concept of outpatient treatment paid for by the employer was untested in Baltimore and only experimented with elsewhere. Third, before an underwriter would reimburse, the clinic would have to be certified as meeting standards, but there was no mechanism for accrediting outpatient alcoholism facilities. Finally, even if health carriers were to offer a plan for outpatient alcoholism treatment benefits, it would have to be approved by the State Insurance Commission.

Development of Third-party Reimbursement

Because each of the three systems held some appeal and no single system became the clear "pretender" to the future financing of the project, all three options had to be pursued throughout the first eighteen months of the project's life. However, early in 1974, through its appointee to the project's advisory board, Blue Cross of Maryland began a preliminary inquiry into the costs of operating EHP and of delivering outpatient alcoholism benefits. Changing Blue Cross' initial interest in outpatient alcoholism treatment into an actual source of funding was a complex and prolonged process, which should be of interest to those who would like to replicate the EHP experience.

The first phase was to develop Blue Cross' commitment to the concept of underwriting outpatient alcoholism services. This task was facilitated in the case of Maryland Blue Cross due to its already high degree of interest in the general problem of alcoholism. Maryland Blue Cross had been the first such carrier in the nation to reimburse impatient care for alcoholics. Through the efforts of both labor and management members of the advisory board and of Blue Cross' appointee to the board, who actively communicated to his superiors the growing consumer interest in outpatient coverage, Blue Cross was alerted to the developing need for a benefit package that would provide to its subscribers outpatient services of the kind offered by EHP. Additionally, several union leaders met with the senior account executives of Maryland Blue Cross and indicated that they were committed to negotiate alcoholism treatment benefits at the next round of contract renewals, covering some 30,000 to 50,000 employees. They requested that Blue Cross prepare rates which could be used in collective bargaining. Thus, EHP contributed to the development of outpatient coverage by presenting persons (unions) ready to purchase services.

Achieving Accreditation

As part of the process of preparing for Blue Cross reimbursement, the clinic has to be formally recognized as providing satisfactory and acceptable care by satisfying the requirements both that the health professionals providing the services be licensed practitioners, and that the delivery institution be accredited by a recognized body of health care providers. Since outpatient alcoholism programs are relative newcomers among health care delivery institutions, at the beginning of the project there was no existing group responsible for certifying such programs. The steps toward solving this problem began in the fall of 1974, when the Joint Commission on Hospital Accreditation (JCHA) announced that it would develop criteria for outpatient alcoholism programs and facilities to be tested on a trial basis in Maryland as well as two other states. Upon this announcement, EHP immediately applied to JCHA for an accreditation evaluation. In March 1975 a two-man team was sent from Chicago to evaluate EHP in terms of 200 preestablished clinical and administrative criteria. The examiners cited the project as being far above the expectations developed by JCHA for outpatient alcoholism programs. EHP received a two-year accreditation certificate and was chosen by JCHA as an unofficial model program.

The EHP Fee Schedule

For the clinic, the most important task involved in developing the third-party payer mechanism was to create a schedule of fees which would be reimbursed by Blue Cross. Since EHP was the only outpatient clinic in the state to work with Blue Cross in developing program benefits, its estimates would have an obvious impact on programs to follow. For this reason, and because the clinic would be forced to maintain itself on its reimbursed fees, great care and study went into preparing the schedule (see table 2-2).

A number of studies have examined program costs of delivering outpatient benefits which help to establish the relative cost-effectiveness of EHP. Table 2-3 gives the cost per patient hour or visit for seven other outpatient alcoholism programs. The range of costs per hour is dramatic, from $10 to $86. At $25 per visit, EHP costs clearly fall at the lower end of the spectrum. It should also be noted that the EHP fees were calculated in 1975 dollars which were more inflated than those used in the other program estimates, the most recent of which were based on 1973 dollars.

Eventually, Blue Cross developed three outpatient alcoholism plans which offered employers and other subscribers a range of benefits, with per individual premiums of $0.08 per month for the least comprehensive and $0.20 for the most comprehensive plan. In September 1975 the State Insurance Commission gave Blue Cross approval to market all three plans for outpatient treatment. On October 1, Blue Cross began a wide-scale publicity aimed at the community at large, with specific promotional efforts directed to its 17,000 employer subscribers.

Future Ownership and Control of EHP

During the spring of 1975, the project's advisory board appointed a subcommittee to consider the question of ownership of the clinic after the university's withdrawal. The subcommittee considered three principal options. The first was a nonprofit community corporation managed by the project's advisory board. This option would have moved the clinic into a fee-for-service financial structure, preserving the staffing pattern that had evolved during the first two years. The second was a nonprofit community corporation which would seek

Table 2-2
The Employee Health Program Patient Fee Schedule

Procedure	Fee[a]	Total
First thirty days		
Treatment plan preparation		
2 Initial interviews	$35	$ 70
1 Physical examination	40	40
1 Psychiatric examination	40	40
1 Physical follow-up	15	15
1 Staff-patient conference	25	25
1 Laboratory test (blood,urine)	25	25
Posttreatment plan counseling		
5 Individual therapy visits	25	125
3 Group therapy visits	15	45
Subsequent visits[b]		
Individual therapy visits	25	500
Group therapy visits	15	300
		$1185

[a]The fees were determined by prorating actual expenses of the several clinical activities across all patients and allowing for a normal period of time in treatment. In the case of physical and psychiatric examinations, the fees represent actual payments to the physicians plus an overhead allowance. Laboratory fees are charged without clinic overhead since they are subcontracted to a laboratory which can bill Blue Cross directly. The fees of $25 for individual counseling and $15 for group therapy reflect true costs plus overhead. These figures were determined by taking all costs less physician and laboratory expenses and dividing by the number of individual and group visits for the six-month period, January 1 through June 30, 1975.

[b]While the number of individual and group visits after the first thirty days may vary, the typical patient would require about twenty individual therapy visits and twenty group therapy sessions.

continuing institutional support for its major financing and would contract for services with a separate corporation composed of the project's treatment staff. The third option was to turn the project over in toto to one of the two groups interested in operating it—the Metropolitan Baltimore AFL-CIO or BACA.

Almost from the start, the committee was destined to choose the third option. The most compelling reason was that such an arrangement would provide for immediate financial sponsorship. Moreover, both BACA and the AFL-CIO displayed enthusiasm, while there was an apparent lack of sponsorship for the other two options. The emergence of BACA and AFL-CIO interest in taking over EHP provides an interesting insight into the project's impact on the community. Throughout the first year of clinic operation, BACA had been increasingly uncomfortable with the role played in the project by organized labor, a concern stemming mainly from its previous favorable experiences with management

Table 2-3
Cost Comparison of Outpatient Alcoholism Programs[a]

Program	Type of Program	Period of Study	Cost per Patient Hour/Visit
Employee Health Program	Employer-Union	January to June, 1975	$25
Providence	HMO-based	March to December, 1973	20
New York City	Municipal Employer	March to December, 1973	80
Washington	Hospital-based	March to December, 1973	71
Rockledge	Mental Health Center-based	March to December, 1973	29
Kalamazoo	Community Drug Program	March to December, 1973	45
Marion	Community Alcoholism Council	March to December, 1973	10

[a]To make EHP estimates comparable with others, an hourly rate had to be chosen. This figure represents one hour of individual therapy at the EHP rate. It is, like the other hourly figures reported, a rate based on actual experience. (From Stanford Research Institute 1974)

interest in alcoholism. Additionally, some management representatives to the advisory board felt a need to form a loose confederation or caucus to counter the natural bond that joined the union representatives from the onset. Although the management caucus seemed to have BACA influence in its bid for project ownership, it never emerged as a controlling force on the advisory board. Management representatives were never empowered by their superiors to commit employer resources; thus, even though the caucus presented the appearance of a cohesive management viewpoint or "interest," it could not act decisively.

The bid by the Baltimore AFL-CIO was grounded in circumstances considerably beyond the scope of the project. During recent years, the organized labor movement has expressed growing concern over its ability to stimulate and influence existing public and private social welfare agencies, voluntary community treatment facilities (e.g., neighborhood health centers), and major hospitals to deliver high-quality care to its members. As a result, the AFL-CIO had decided to organize a number of such activities under a union aegis called the Community Service Agency (CSA). CSA was incorporated in early 1975 and began to plan various projects. Since the director of CSA was also a member of the advisory board and one of the initiators of the EHP experiment, it was only natural that CSA set out to take on the project as its first activity. The board's attraction to this option was that CSA proposed to leave the EHP plan virtually intact, and would continue the advisory board in its present mix of labor and management. The BACA plan, on the other hand, implied to union leaders a change in operating goals, that is, making the project somehow more responsive to management. The AFL-CIO plan was endorsed by the advisory board in July 1975, and plans for the University's divestiture on behalf of CSA were put into effect.

In retrospect, the CSA plan was bound to win out over BACA's bid for a number of reasons. First, the AFL-CIO pledged itself to full financial support of the project at the advisory board meeting in July. BACA was in no position to make a similar guarantee. Second, the management caucus was not displeased in any discernible way with how the program was being operated and, thus, any attempt to form the management representatives into an effective dissident group would be likely to fail. Third, the union representatives had repeatedly displayed both unquestionable loyalty to the program and genuine fairness in all issues debated by advisory council. A spirit of good faith and trust linked the union members of the council who had seen the project through hard times and had been jointly pleased with the project's emerging predominance. Finally, the AFL-CIO proposal defused any management objection by providing for a continuing role for management representatives in the policymaking board of EHP.

As the project closed its second year of operation, its future looked both secure and bright. It would be taken over by the community and was enjoying both a local and national reputation for excellent treatment. Everything proceeded as planned and on October 31, 1975, the university turned control of the project over to CSA.

EHP continued to operate under the aegis of CSA until the fall of 1976, when insufficient funds forced the clinic to close. Despite the success of the project in laying the groundwork for long-term financing (through development of Blue Cross reimbursement coverage), there were insufficient short-term funds to support clinic activities until such time as the reimbursement mechanism could become capable of supporting total operating costs.

The Blue Cross outpatient package was not marketed until October 1975, and although the benefits have attracted many subscribers, extension of coverage to a sufficient number of workers to sustain the clinic did not occur soon enough. Many EHP employers had been in fixed contracts with Blue Cross and could not purchase the new services until their present contracts had expired and new ones could be negotiated. It is likely that, had the clinic been able to continue for about two years under CSA management, all referred patients would have been covered by the Blue Cross plans of their employers. Government funds remaining after the demonstration phase were sufficient to operate the clinic only for about six months. After that period, the AFL-CIO paid for the clinic out of its own reserves. No other support was forthcoming either from government or from the participating employers. Unable to continue providing all of the interim funding needed, the CSA had to close the clinic, and EHP patients were then shifted over to the alcoholism program of the Johns Hopkins Hospital.

3

Identification and Referral

In the main, conventional settings for treating alcoholics or problem drinkers, be they outpatient clinics, hospital detoxification wards, halfway houses, or the psychiatrist's couch, are sponsored, run, and their clientele generated by the therapeutic community. By contrast, in industrial alcoholism programs, the identification and referral of patients must depend largely on individuals and organizations for whom such a role is at the most secondary. Indeed, the tasks involved in implementing any new occupational health program are formidable, regardless of how enthusiastically supported by management and union. Should a new program identify and label workers as alcoholic, the problems increase geometrically, acceptance of alcoholism as a disease notwithstanding. It is not surprising, therefore, that much of what is written on industrial alcoholism programs is devoted to the problems and interactions of the parties involved in identification and referral.

The Employee Health Program (EHP) offered to participating companies the benefits of past experience, both successes and failures. Model policies, procedures, and guidelines were made available, as was continuing assistance to carry them out in the form of liaison personnel and clinic staff. But the literature on industrial alcoholism abounds with problems and complexities which confound the best laid plans, and EHP was no exception. In establishing and operating the program, EHP grappled with a range of problems by now familiar—union-management cooperation, institutional and individual barriers to identification and referral, ambiguities in policy—multiplied by twelve.

Establishing a treatment facility shared by several employers and unions with conflicting intents and expectations proved to be the most difficult of the project's demonstration goals. Since successful institutionalization of the identification and referral process was accomplished despite the clinic's ultimate closing, EHP's experiences in attempting to improve the referral capabilities of the parties are among its most instructive.

Components of the Identification and Referral Process

EHP advocated the constructive confrontation technique as the preferred method of identification and referral on the basis of its demonstrated effectiveness in other programs. (The therapeutic value of the constructive confrontation technique is discussed in chaper 4.) In fact, some EHP participants had alcoholism programs in existence prior to becoming participants that incorporated many of the features described below. Keeping in mind that each firm differed in its precise approach to identification and referral, and that the approach used in practice often differs from the ideal, the following description summarizes the main features of the approach preferred by most of the participants.

By far the most frequent means used by EHP participating companies to identify employees with potential drinking problems was through a supervisor who had observed a deterioration in work performance or attendance, although some participating firms also relied on examination of attendance records, supervisory evaluations, and medical claims records.

Once an employee had been identified as a likely problem drinker, the identifying individual or department was responsible for accumulating written evidence of deficient work performance or behavior with which to confront the worker. During the confrontation, which was often preceded by a series of warnings, the record of unsatisfactory performance was presented to the employee, along with the admonition that he must improve. At this point, the employee was encouraged to seek help for any problem that may have been contributing to his poor performance, and EHP was suggested as one option among others. While it was made clear to the employee that his acceptance of treatment would not hinder his job security or chances for promotion, he was made to understand that if he did not seek help and his performance did not improve, he would be subject to discipline or discharge as specified in the collective bargaining agreement or in the (written or tacit) personnel policy guidelines. Where possible, the supervisor did not mention any suspicion that the problem was alcoholism, consistent with the restriction of the supervisor's role to documentation of impaired performance. Additionally, this served to minimize the danger that the employee could look upon the confrontation as an unwarranted intrusion into his personal life or habits.

If, upon confrontation, the employee decided to take advantage of the help offered, he was sent to the coordinating department or individual within the company for referral to treatment. The coordinator again emphasized that treatment was being offered without penalty, consistent with the company's attitude that alcoholism is a disease and that help is made available as a part of the employee's medical benefits. Additionally, and vital to his acceptance of and continued participation in treatment, the worker was assured of a strict policy of confidentiality regarding the confrontation, referral, and the nature of help being offered.

Upon agreeing to participate in EHP, most employers reserved the right to refer workers to other treatment facilities if they deemed it advisable or if the confronted worker so insisted. Employers were also free to permit employees to seek counseling with a clergyman or to get help from their physician. This freedom protected the employer from appearing despotic in his rehabilitation plans. Thus, as will be discussed again later on, the EHP case load represented only a portion of the individuals confronted under the employers' policies. If the parties did agree upon EHP, the referring person made an appointment for the worker as soon as possible, in order to maintain the immediacy of the confrontation encounter. After the first visit, the clinic assumed the major responsibility for securing attendance. Once in treatment, the employee's progress was tracked by the referring individual.

Since the cooperation and goodwill of the union is essential to the effectiveness of any industrial alcoholism program (Belasco et al. 1969), union representatives were informed of the referral by most participating employers as a matter of policy, and participated in follow-up procedures. Additionally, through union liaison personnel, EHP encouraged union representatives to take an active role in the confrontation and referral process, and devoted considerable resources in educating them in identification of potential problem drinkers as well as in cooperating with management to facilitate referrals.

Since self-referrals avoid the necessity for the lengthy confrontation episode, it was the policy of most EHP firms to make known to their entire work forces their participation in the program and the availability of the treatment option for any worker who perceived himself to be in need of help for a drinking problem. Among the EHP survey population, 12 percent were self-referrals, not an insubstantial figure, considering that they were among the first workers referred to the program.

While most EHP participating employers attempted to follow the constructive confrontation method outlined above, they differed in two major ways. First, since the Employee Health Program existed as an outside treatment plan, each employer had to establish an organizational mechanism for referring workers to treatment. Figure 3-1 shows the five types of organizational mechanisms which emerged among the participating employers. Type 1, in which equilateral power to refer was vested in both the employer's medical and personnel departments, was the most common referral mechanisms used by EHP participating firms. In type 2 organizations, referral was controlled by the personnel department, which sent referred workers to the medical department, if necessary, before referring out. In type 3 organizations, the medical department controlled referrals to the clinic. In each of the above three systems, independent referral by a union representative was possible. The fourth organizational type was used by only one participating employer. Here, a subdivision of the personnel department—employee counseling—made referrals. Finally, the fifth type was the labor-management cooperative model, also found in only one of the project's employers. This employer had a joint-management alcoholism committee before the inception of the project, and used EHP as its exclusive treatment resource after it became a participant. All five of the organizational types allowed for self-identification and self-referral.

The second area in which the companies diverged was in the breadth of problems or services offered under their alcoholism policy. While ten of the

Type 1: Equilateral Medical/Personnel

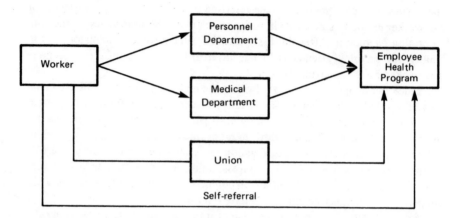

Type 2: Personnel Department Dominant

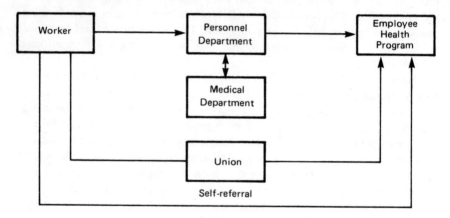

Type 3: Medical Department Dominant

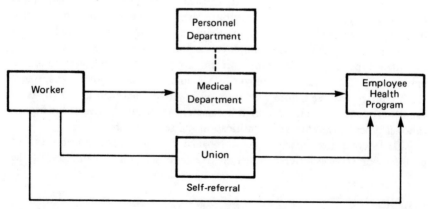

Type 4: Counseling Intermediary Dominant

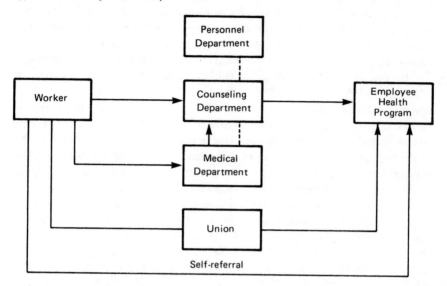

Type 5: Labor/Management Cooperation

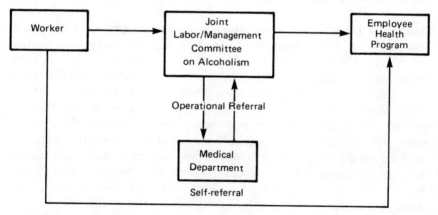

Figure 3-1. Organizational Flow of Identified Alcoholics among Participating Employers.

participating companies only referred workers thought to have a drinking problem, the programs of two participating companies were based on the "employee assistance concept" (the broad-brush approach), in which workers were referred to treatment to correct poor job performance, whatever the cause. The employee counseling subdivision described above was one such employee assistance program.

Because all but one participating employer referred workers to treatment in addition to EHP, it was impossible to judge which organizational model or which breadth of program services was most effective in referring workers to treatment. However, project experience did underscore the importance of having at least one individual in each company who was responsible for and committed to the alcoholism program and capable of tempering the inherent conflicts between management and union. Thus, in those companies where resources, principally in the form of a person specifically assigned to deal with alcoholism problems, have been committed at adequate levels, referrals were made routinely, regardless of organizational type. Conversely, experience showed that in companies having no staff member charged with facilitating clinic-company interaction, referral was impossible, regardless of the announced commitment of cooperation with the project from the highest levels within the organization.

Labor and Management Liaison Efforts

Analysts of industrial alcoholism programs point to the importance of training supervisory and union personnel regarding their responsibilities in implementing the program (Trice and Belasco 1966, 1968). As a consequence, EHP invested considerable resources in developing labor and management liaison officers and in educating them in efforts to stimulate referrals. As described earlier, the tasks of the labor liaison staff included the presentation of a periodic and frequent program "presence" among the participating unions, providing education for union stewards about the project and, when necessary, facilitating individual referrals. Similar tasks were performed by the management liaison staff among potential referring sources (agents) and the participating employer organizations. In short, the project's liaison personnel were charged with the task of ensuring a constant flow of referrals during the first eighteen months of clinic life.

Table 3-1 shows the number of referrals to the program by company during the first twenty-six months of clinic operations as well as the full-time equivalent liaison manpower expended. As shown in the table, during the first seven months, one management and one union liaison person were employed. Over the next twelve months, in an effort to stimulate more referrals, the manpower devoted to liaison efforts was doubled. Finally, during the last seven months, liaison efforts were cut back to one part-time management person and one full-time labor liaison. The average monthly referral rates were 9 in the first seven months, 14 in the first and 20 in the second half of 1974, and 18 in the last seven months.

Table 3-1
Referral Pattern to the Employee Health Program by Company and Liaison Manpower Efforts (1973 to 1975)

Number of New Referrals

Company	1973: J-J	A	S	O	N	D	1974: J	F	M	A	M	J	J	A	S	O	N	D	1975: J	F	M	A	M	J	J
A								2[a]	1												1	1	1		
B						2										5	5	2	2	3	6	7	8	7	
C	3[a]	2	5	5	7	1	3	1	2	1	2	5	9	10	12	6	6	5	6	7	2		2		9
D					1	4	2	4	1	1	1	2	1	1	1	2	1	2	2						3
E							4[a]		1	2	2	1	1	1	1	1								2	5
F	1[a]						1	1		1	1														
G	1[a]	2	2																					1	
H	1[a]			3	1	1										2	2	2							1
I	2[a]			3	1	2	3	2	1	2	2	1	1	5	2	3	2	3			2	3	1	2	
J				1[a]	2	1	4	4	3	4	1	1	1	2		1	2	2	1	1			2		
K	4[a]		1	3	2	1	2		3	2	2	2	1	1	3	1	1	3	1	2		1			1
L												1[a]	1	2	1					4	3	5	9	1	
M[b]												1[a]	1						3	3				3	3
Total	12	4	8	15	13	11	19	14	12	12	11	15	15	25	17	18	24	22	15	17	14	17	23	16	22

[a]Indicates first month when company could have referred patients pursuant to letter of participation.

[b]Nonmember companies.

Management liaison efforts

Labor liaison efforts

(Each line = one full-time liaison worker.)

Thus, as discussed in chapter 2, the referral mechanism was sufficiently routinized by January 1975 that referrals showed no appreciable decline despite the cutback in liaison activity.

In anticipation of comparing each company's referral rates according to the degree of management-liaison activity expended by the project, each liaison officer was required to keep a log of his activities. Table 3-2 shows referrals by employer according to man-months of management-liaison activity. While 2.9 man-years (or 5800 man-hours) of liaison efforts were expended, only 55 percent of man-hours can be clearly connected to liaison with specific employers. The balance of liaison time was spent on such general activities as staff meetings and training efforts, which might be said to have benefited all management referral efforts.

Table 3-2 shows a wide range of referral rates among the participating employers, from a high of 0.46 per 100 man-months at risk for company E to a low of 0.04 for agency K. Given that the number of referrals from each employer is so small compared to the work force at risk, it is not surprising that the resultant ranking of employers largely reflects the size of the companies' work forces, thus obscuring the relationship between referral rates and liaison activity.

Aside from the influence of diverging purposes and philosophies among employers on the rate of referrals, several factors render measuring the impact of liaison activities difficult. Table 3-2 shows great disparity in the pattern of liaison hours by size of employer and actual referral activity. This reflects the inability of liaison personnel to gain access to several employer organizations as well as an a priori judgment on how much liaison work was appropriate. For example, management at company C rejected periodic intrusion by liaison personnel, and the 340 hours expended there represent the facilitation of specific referrals rather than supervisory training programs and the like. Furthermore, it is impossible to control for the effect of referral to non-EHP treatment options in assessing the impact of liaison activity. Indeed, the table shows that firms producing the fewest referrals to EHP relative to their work forces at risk, are those having their own in-house management or union programs.

Despite the fact that no apparent relationship exists between man-hours of liaison activity and referral rates by company, it would nevertheless be misleading to discount the value of the liaison efforts. All four employers having in-house programs repeatedly indicated the spillover effect of EHP liaison activity in the form of increased referrals to their programs. Similarly, other community treatment programs received referrals as a result of EHP liaison efforts. For example, one company often offered the referred employee the option of treatment in the Baltimore County alcoholism outpatient program which was located much closer to it than was the EHP clinic.

Table 3–2
Referrals by Employer in Man-months (June 1973–July 1975)

Company	Referrals per 100 Man-months	3200 Logged-hours of Management Liaison Activity[a]	Number of Employees	Months in Program	Total Referrals	Treatment Provided by Employer or Union
E	0.46	400 (2, 3, 4)	647	26	8	No
D	0.42	130 (10)	3,650	20	31	No
G	0.35	80 (12)	429	26	4	No
A	0.26	150 (8, 9)	1,037	18	5	No
F	0.25	100 (11)	1,190	26	8	No
C	0.24	340 (5)	21,119	26	134	No
L	0.19	400 (2, 3, 4)	6,252	26	31	Yes
B	0.07	400 (2, 3, 4)	8,067	26	16	No
J	0.07	300 (6)	20,961	26	42	No
H	0.06	150 (8, 9)	6,015	14	5	Yes
I	0.06	250 (7)	18,372	19	22	Yes
K	0.04	500 (1)	42,445	18	35	Yes

[a]Represents 55 percent of all man-hours logged. Figures in parentheses indicate rank of company in increasing order of liaison effort expended.

The Supervisor and the Referral Process

As noted above, the project's management liaison personnel conducted periodic supervisory education sessions and also made reports to supervisors to inform them of a referred patient's attendance and progress at the clinic. Recognizing the key role of first-line supervision in the identification and referral process, Trice and Roman (1972) state:

> The supervisor's position in the organization allows detection of developing deviance, and the closeness of first-line supervisors' relations with their charges sets the stage for effective actions toward the deviant. The supervisor's effectiveness is determined by five factors: his knowledge of the signs of deviant drinking and drug use, his knowledge of company policy regarding deviant drinkers and drug users, his willingness to implement those company policies, his firmness in implementing the policies, and his consistency in following through.

Because EHP fashioned its referral system around the supervisor as the primary identification and referral person, the five factors mentioned by Trice and Roman as important to his effectiveness were made the foundation of the supervisory training program.

To gain some insight into the impact of these education and training efforts, and to obtain a sense of how the referral process actually took place, interviews were conducted in the spring of 1975 with eighteen supervisors who had participated in twenty referrals to EHP. The modal supervisor was a white male, forty-five years old with two years of college. He had been with his agency or company for fifteen years, had been a supervisor for ten years, and he supervised fifty employees. Among the twenty workers referred by the supervisors, were one professional, three clerical workers, two operatives, one skilled craftsman, four laborers, and nine service workers. Twelve of the referred workers were black and eight were white. The supervisors—two from company E, four from agency I, and twelve from agency K—were questioned about (1) how they identified the worker as presenting a problem; (2) what they did about it with respect to their company's policy governing referral of problem drinkers; and (3) their attitudes toward the policy and the impact of treatment on the worker. In the hope of encouraging frank expression of opinion, the supervisors were not told of the interviewer's connection to the Employee Health Program, but only that the survey was being conducted for Johns Hopkins University. Although these interview data come from a very small, nonrepresentative sample of EHP supervisors, their consistency with the findings of an important study conducted by Trice and Beyer (1977) of a random sample of supervisors in seventy-one federal civil service installations makes them of more general interest than would otherwise be the case.

Identification

The supervisors were asked two questions to determine how they identified a worker as a problem drinker: What factors make an employee a problem for you in general? What, if any, on-the-job problems led you to identify the worker as needing a referral? Table 3-3 lists the responses to the first question, and table 3-4 lists the problems of the seventeen workers who presented on-the-job problems to their supervisors. The tables show that whereas absenteeism, lateness, or impaired performance were the most frequently cited general problems (one or more of these three problems was mentioned by sixteen supervisors), only four supervisors said that absenteeism or performance was the main factor in actually identifying a referred worker, even though declining performance was the preferred basis for identification of a worker adopted by all three companies where the interviews were conducted. As shown in table 3-4, the problem that most often brought a referred worker to the attention of his supervisor was his "drinking," "alcoholism," or "habit." Drinking was mentioned as the main or secondary problem of eleven of the sixteen workers having on-the-job problems, and of the six employees whose supervisors did not mention drinking as a problem leading to identification, alcoholism was thought to be the underlying cause of the problems of all but one of them.

Since these workers were among the first to be identified under their companies' programs, one would expect their drinking problems to be at a relatively advanced stage. And because alcoholics are among the most visible of problem employees (Trice and Roman 1972), it is not surprising that so many supervisors saw the problem as drinking per se rather than its effects on

Table 3-3
Responses to the Question: What Factors Make an Employee a Problem for You in General?

Problem	Number of Times Mentioned
Absenteeism and sick leave abuse	13
Tardiness	9
Poor productivity/performance	8
Drinking on the job	6
Insubordination; improper conduct	6
Coming to work hungover or intoxicated	3
Personal problems	2
Disrupting others' work	2
Safety/accidents	2
Lazy; unmotivated	2
Theft	1

Table 3-4
Responses to the Question: What on-the-Job Problems Led You to Identify the Worker as Needing a Referal?[a]

Main Problem	Secondary Problem	Number of Referrals
Drinking/alcoholism	–	5
Drinking/alcoholism	Absenteeism/performance	2
Absenteeism/performance	–	4
Belligerent/hard-to-handle	Drinking/alcoholism	3
Belligerent/hard-to-handle	–	2
No problem	–	4

[a]Workers who presented no on-the-job problems to their supervisors included one who was identified through a communication from the courts regarding a drunk-driving arrest, and two who told their supervisors that they had a drinking problem and asked to be referred to treatment.

work performance. Additionally, Trice and Beyer found that the frequency of using poor performance as a criterion for deciding that an employee had a drinking problem declined, and the frequency of using other observed behavior increased, with increasing proportions of unskilled employees in the civil service installations they studied.

More interesting is the frequency with which belligerence and insubordination were mentioned as problems (a primary or secondary factor in one-third of the referrals). By contrast, in a comparison of factors motivating them to refer psychotic, neurotic, and alcoholic employees, Trice (1965b) found that supervisors of alcoholic workers did not report one factor associated with other types of problem employees: "He was often surly, arrogant, and defiant." However, in Maxwell's survey (1960) of self-reported on-the-job drinking signs, 44 percent of problem-drinking respondents indicated that aggressive feelings or actions toward fellow workers was a serious or moderate problem for them. Because all six of the EHP workers who presented such problems were black, and because an obvious way for a worker to single himself out as a problem is through belligerent or aggressive behavior, further study of the relationship between this factor and the race or ethnicity of referred workers might provide some insight into the nature of the identification process. It is possible that subcultural styles of expression related to drinking (McClelland et al. 1972; Harper 1976) may be a factor contributing to the visibility and thus referral of some workers to industrial alcoholism programs.

Another suggestion for further investigation is shown in table 3-5, which indicates that no white male worker was referred by a black male supervisor. It would be interesting to discover whether a sample of sufficient size would yield a similar pattern.

Table 3-5
Race of Supervisor by Race of Referred Worker

Supervisors	Referred Workers[a]	
	White Male	Black Male
White male	5	5
Black male	–	6
White female	–	1
Black female	1	–

[a]Excludes two workers who requested their own referrals.

Company Policy and Referral

The supervisors were also asked what steps they took once the employee became a problem, and, in order to determine their familiarity with the employer's policy and how it influenced their behavior in making the referral, they were asked to state their perception of the nature of their employer's alcoholism policy.

At the time that interviews were being conducted, company E and its employees' union had agreed upon and were following a comprehensive alcoholism policy which they planned to make official during upcoming collective bargaining negotiations. That policy, understood by both company E supervisors interviewed, specified that the supervisor was to confront the worker with documentation of impaired performance and then to refer him to the personnel or medical department. One company E supervisor brought the problem to the attention of the personnel department without even speaking to the worker, and the second attempted to counsel the worker, but referred him to the medical department when the worker denied that he had been drinking.

Among all EHP participating firms and agencies, agency K had the most comprehensive alcoholism policy and program for its employees, the components of which were specified in detail in its personnel policy statements. The agency's policy stated that supervisors were to refer any worker who manifested poor work performance to the agency's employee counseling service, either immediately upon recognition of a work problem or after confronting the worker with documentation of poor performance. It was the responsiblity of the employee counseling service to offer treatment to the worker. Of the twelve supervisors from agency K, nine were familiar with and understood the agency's policy, and the three who did not, consulted their own supervisors about what action to take when the worker became a problem. Before referring the problem worker to the counseling service, one agency K supervisor transferred his employee, a professional social worker, to "a less sensitive assignment," and two attempted to counsel the worker themselves. The remaining nine agency K supervisors referred the worker directly to the counseling service, taking no additional action.

In contrast to the personnel policy statements of agency K, in which the procedures for referral were explicitly stated, the agreement between agency I and its employees' union stated only that agency-trained counseling officers (union representatives) were responsible for counseling employees with "problems such as alcoholism," and that workers could be referred either to an agency counseling program or to other appropriate treatment resources. Although the agency did send periodic memoranda to supervisors regarding its policy of attempting to retain problem-drinking workers who accepted the treatment option, the agreement did not specify how referral to treatment was to be made. Not surprisingly, therefore, agency I supervisors showed more variation both in what they did about problem drinkers and in their understanding of the policy than did agency K supervisors.

All four agency I supervisors attempted to counsel the employee. Two then referred the worker to the counseling officer, one (who had two problem employees) fired the men and informed the counseling officer that they would be rehired only if they accepted treatment, and one consulted the counseling officer after first attempting to cover up for the worker. While all four were aware of the counseling officers and of the treatment option, they had differing understandings of the agency's policy. One expressed bewilderment about referring "another man who needs attention," because "each month I get a different memo." The others expressed uncertainty of who was responsible for making the referral to treatment. Only one supervisor, ironically the man who fired his workers, was aware of the agency's policy to keep the man on the job during treatment.

Ten supervisors, distributed evenly among the three employers, reported attempting to follow up on the progress of the worker after the referral. Eight felt that the matter was largely out of their hands once they had made the referral. Of the twenty workers referred, all but three were still employed at the time of the interviews, nine were either still active EHP patients or had received planned discharges from treatment, and eight had dropped out of treatment. Since the active patients were evenly divided between supervisors who followed their progress in treatment and those who did not, it is impossible to attribute any specific therapeutic effect to supervisory follow-up on the basis of this small sample.

It is interesting to note that only three supervisors (one from agency I and two from agency K) had prepared written documentation of poor performance or had sent warning letters to the employees. This may reflect both a tendency, noted by Trice and Beyer, for supervisors of lower-status employees to judge oral forms of communication as more effective, as well as a trend (especially in agency K) toward making documentation a function of the personnel department. Also interesting is the fact that, despite the policy of all three employers that the supervisor avoid mentioning a suspicion of alcoholism, the majority of supervisors, including some who did not attempt to counsel the worker before making a referral, found it impossible to avoid mentioning that they thought the worker had a drinking problem. Five supervisors who did comply strictly with this aspect of the policy admitted that they delayed a long time before taking action, waiting until the employee's work performance had deteriorated so badly that no explanation was needed for making the referral.

Attitudes toward the Policy and Treatment

On the basis of the supervisors' responses, it appears that the majority of them attempted to comply with their employer's policy as they understood it. Only two supervisors, one who tried to cover up and one who fired his workers, admitted to having acted against the guidelines. All but four of the supervisors felt that the policy was a good one overall, mentioning primarily humanitarian concerns, such as "it gives the person a chance" (nine supervisors), for approving of the program. Only one mentioned the more utilitarian reason of saving the worker "for business reasons, making him more productive." Four supervisors gave positive experiences with the program as their reason for approving it. Indeed, of the twenty workers who were referred, the supervisors felt that sixteen had improved as a result of treatment. Not surprisingly, three of the supervisors who did not endorse the policy noticed either no improvement or a worsening in their employee's work subsequent to referral.

This overall approval of the policy does not mean, however, that the supervisors necessarily agreed with all aspects of the policy. When asked what changes they would make in their employer's policy, only three said that they would not make any changes; two felt that they were not sufficiently familiar with the policy to offer an opinion. Of the thirteen who did find fault with one or more features of the policy, nine (half of all the supervisors interviewed) felt that it was too lenient or indirect. One respondent—the only supervisor of a high-level employee that was interviewed—thought that the worker should not be allowed to retain decision-making power while in treatment. The remaining eight (representing all three employers) felt that the policy inhibited early referral to treatment. Some of their responses were as follows:

If I could have referred him earlier, it would have been good. Under the rules you can't do anything if they deny it [alcoholism].

[They should] use force to make a guy join the program. Threatening doesn't work when a guy is low.

Can't say anything about alcohol. We used to be able to counsel them and nip the problem in the bud.

I wish there was a way to detect it sooner and get more authority before it gets too strong. They should be stricter in the beginning.

I would force them to go into the program or refuse them employment. Only when I fired them did they go.

Of the remaining four who had complaints with their employer's policy, two felt that it was too ambiguous or vague (both agency I supervisors), and two complained about not getting feedback from the employee counseling service (agency K supervisors).

Conclusions from Supervisor Interviews

In summary, three general conclusions emerge from this examination of supervisors' practices and attitudes toward identification and referral. First, EHP supervisors tended to hold favorable attitudes toward the provision of treatment for problem-drinking workers, and to show little reluctance in referring them. The majority of supervisors were aware of their employer's alcoholism policy and were, in general, supportive of its existence and objectives. In their study of supervisors in federal installations, Trice and Beyer found that supervisors of relatively low-skill-level workers were more favorable in their assessments of the alcoholism policy and more familiar with its provisions than were supervisors of high-status employees. Although we lack comparable data on supervisors of high-status workers, the behavior and attitudes of EHP supervisors—having primarily low-skill-level service workers under their direction—are meaningful in light of Trice and Beyer's findings.

A second finding from the interviews is the high proportion of EHP supervisors who felt that their employer's policy discouraged early treatment for workers, and that the confrontation tactic centered around work performance as the sole basis for referral actually impeded the referral process. Indeed, given the prevalence of this feeling among EHP supervisors, it is conceivable that in making future referrals more will be tempted to bend the policy especially in light of their positive attitudes toward treatment and the improvement they saw in their workers after the referral.

Finally, the supervisor interviews show the beneficial effect of a comprehensive, written company policy in achieving consistency in the identification and referral process. For agency K supervisors, having a set of specified procedures and guidelines, referral appeared to be a relatively straightforward and uncomplicated experience. This finding should come as no surprise to anyone familiar with the literature on company alcoholism programs, as the existence of a formal written policy is almost universally mentioned as a key ingredient in successful identification and referral efforts (Cline 1975; Presnall 1967). Trice and Roman (1972) note that a written policy is especially useful to the supervisor because it spells out the distribution of authority and responsibility involved in policy implementation. Since only five EHP employers had such a written policy, it is likely that for the majority of supervisors who were not interviewed, the identification and referral experience was more similar to that reported by agency I than by agency K supervisors. Consequently, as will be discussed in a subsequent section of this chapter, EHP hoped to promote the adoption of policy guidelines by participating employers and unions in the form of collective bargaining language.

Effecting Union-Management Cooperation

A major demonstration goal of the project was to develop labor-management cooperation within each company on the question of alcoholism in the work force. Investigators who have studied the problem of securing union coopera- tion in company programs have pointed to basic philosophical differences in how management and labor view industrial alcoholism programs. While manage- ment is usually encouraged to adopt programs on the basis of cost-benefit arguments about gains in productivity and the expense of replacing long-tenured workers, labor views rehabilitation efforts primarily as a means to protect the jobs of its members, and thus as a broadening of their health benefits (Roman and Trice 1976).

Clearly, with such different attitudes toward the value or importance of treatment, each party could be expected to view the other's participation in EHP with a certain amount of suspicion. In the precontract negotiations, the primary concern of employers was that by cooperating with labor in a program designed primarily to retain the jobs of alcoholic workers, management would participate in an informal process involving potential circumscription of its right to discipline or fire alcoholic workers who have traditionally presented many problems. On the other hand, the most consistently raised concern by union leaders was that alcohol abuse would be used as an excuse to discharge troublesome employees.

Another fear expressed by management was that if it were to recognize a different disciplinary procedure for workers identified as alcoholic, whether expressed in unilateral management policy statements or in collective bargaining contract language, the union would protest many firings on the grounds that the employee was an alcoholic and thus deserving of protection under the policy. Interestingly, this objection did not prove to be an overriding one in the pre- planning stage, since unions do not welcome grievance handling and arbitration procedures for alcoholic workers any more than management does. Prospec- tive EHP unions mentioned that such efforts often turn out to have been wasted in light of repeat offenses that result in the employee's termination at some later date. Therefore, unions saw the project's goal of early treatment and rehabilitation as a way to produce a lasting change in work performance that could preclude such confrontation altogether.

The labor-management differences were ultimately resolved with an understanding that EHP worked out between the parties, that is, management made an informal commitment not to fire a worker undergoing treatment, and to cooperate with the union in developing contractually binding language that would specify the conditions under which workers could be fired for alcohol-related behaviors. While the vision of the union thus cooperating with management in a program to identify workers as alcoholics created some uneasiness for union leadership, by stressing the help-without-penalty provision, they could be effective in retaining workers who management might otherwise fire. To secure management acceptance of this resolution, EHP offered employers free treatment for workers in exchange for a twofold commitment: they would make every effort to retain workers who were undergoing treatment without in any way compromising their ultimate right to fire, and would provide work history data on referred workers for the research goals of the project.[1]

Before discussing how the union-management relationship evolved in actual experience, it is useful to summarize some major ways in which EHP differed from most industrial alcoholism programs, which are sponsored by single firms. The decision to adopt industrial alcoholism programs is usually made by management—although often with outside encouragement[2]—based on its belief that treatment represents a sound investment in its work force. Though sentiments of corporate responsibility toward workers frequently emerge, the initial motivation is usually economic. Additionally, all the expenses of mounting and operating the program are almost always borne by the employer. The union is involved as a secondary, cooperating party. A written policy statement on the program is drafted, often with union input, and circulated throughout the organization. Finally, there is usually a tacit or written commitment that the policy will be applied comprehensively throughout the work force, without regard to occupational status or rank. Most often identified workers are referred to outside agencies for treatment.[3]

EHP differed from the above model in several ways. Being a multiemployer program, it represented a variety of management motivations and expectations. While EHP certainly contributed to the companies' interest in the problem of alcohol in the work place, corporatewide commitments at the national level contributed to the decisions of many employers to participate in the program. Some, notably the localized nonunion companies, appeared to be motivated primarily by humanitarian concerns. Others already had operating programs and used EHP as an additional referral source. Another major difference was that unions were to be a coequal party in the EHP program and to participate with management in the identification and referral mechanism. With respect to the existence of *written* policy guidelines, only six companies had collective bargaining language or policy statements on alcohol or the treatment of alcoholic workers; thus, for many employers, participation in EHP became their de factor policy on alcoholism. Moreover, there were no provisions for uniform application of the policy across all employee status levels in the work force.

Finally, and it could be argued most importantly, the decision of employers to participate in EHP represented a different order of commitment to alcoholism identification and referral from that implied by a single company's decision to initiate and finance a program. It seems only natural that even a management strongly committed to rehabilitation would have a greater stake in the success of a program that it controls than one in which it only participates.

Labor, Management, and the Referral Process

Even though the project devoted considerable resources to promoting labor-management cooperation and to improving the identification and referral capabilities of participating firms, referrals to the clinic never reached anticipated levels. Thus, in twenty-six months of clinic operation 391 patients had been referred, 150 patients or 30 percent fewer than the project's projection of 250 patients annually. While several factors contributing to the low level of referrals to the clinic have already been identified in this and the previous chapter, an additional factor may have been the predominantly blue-collar makeup of EHP's case load. Thus, as will be discussed again in Chapter 5, the clinic drew from only a limited segment of the potential population of problem drinkers in the companies' work forces. Recognizing that the policy of offering an identified worker a range of treatment options might result in employers sending higher-level workers elsewhere (e.g., private physicians or hospitals), EHP requested that all participating companies and unions supply the project with details of the procedures that were followed with all workers who came to their attention through the identification process, including both those who were referred elsewhere as well as those who refused treatment. Because the project had no success in obtaining such information, it is not known how many workers were actually referred for alcoholism treatment, or how an employee's occupational status related to the type of treatment he received. However, in light of the experiences of many company alcoholism programs reported in the literature (Trice and Roman 1972; Warkov et al. 1965), it seems likely that many higher-level alcoholic employees—whose job performance is less visible to supervision than that of blue-collar workers—escaped identification altogether.

Serving primarily the goals of research into the work force behavior of referred workers rather than as an attempt to reach the maximum number of problem drinkers in the population at risk, the project took no specific measures to resolve the problem of hard-to-identify problem drinkers, nor did it apply pressure on employers to refer higher-level workers. However, the de facto identify of EHP as a blue-collar treatment facility had consequences beyond limiting the number of workers referred to the clinic. Indeed, if one factor were to be singled out to explain the great interest and eventual takeover of the clinic by the AFL-CIO's Community Service Agency, it would be that 90 percent of workers referred to EHP were members of collective bargaining units.

But even though organized labor appeared to be more enthusiastic about the EHP concept than most of the participating employers, the reluctance of union representatives to refer early was another factor why referrals failed to reach anticipated levels. Thus, despite the fact that union officials were empowered to initiate a confrontation and referral, the great majority of union referrals made to EHP took place only after other attempts at assistance had failed. Of 172 of the EHP study population referred to the clinic by employers or unions, over one-third were union referrals. Analysis of the work history forms and responses of patients on the intake questionnaire revealed that five out of six of these union referrals were made either to stave off or to reverse a termination decision. Of twenty-four workers who arrived at the clinic having already been suspended, twenty-one were referred via a union representative.

Several reasons appear to have influenced union reluctance to initiate a referral, the overriding one being political. Local union officials must stand periodically for reelection and an incumbent's identification of members as alcoholics could become an issue. Local union leaders had stated this concern to the researchers repeatedly, along with another fear—that by going on record as having identified a comember's poor work record they would risk being called by an arbitrator to testify against the worker should an employer seek to terminate him at some future time. This phenomenon also suggests that a considerable proportion of these referrals had drinking problems that were in a relatively advanced stage. Clearly, the sizable proportion of referrals which can be shown to have been near termination indicates that the goal of early identification did not materialize, at least for the first set of referred workers.

When viewed in light of the number of union referrals, it would appear that management barriers also played a part in the referral rates experienced by EHP. While many factors serving to limit referrals have already been mentioned in this and the previous chapter, table 3-6, which shows for each employer the percentage of all referrals by quarterly period of participation in the project, offers some additional suggestions. Of the twelve employers listed, for only two did referrals consistently increase with longer participation in the project. Seven employers made the greatest number of referrals in the earliest period of their involvement in the program, five of whom showed a consistent decrease in the number of referrals over time. One explanation for this finding is the tendency for the most easily identifiable problem drinkers to be referred first. To identify borderline cases, the supervisor not only must expend more effort but is also more likely to experience ambivalence, especially regarding a worker who is productive in general, despite occasional lapses. Indeed, many employers were not committed to raising "alcoholism consciousness" in their

Table 3-6

Employers by Percentage of Referrals in Quarterly Periods (June 1973-June 1975)

	Percentage of Referrals by Quarterly Period[a]				
Company	(1)	(2)	(3)	(4)	Number
A	*	60.0	40.0	00.0	5
B	*	12.5	37.5	50.0	16
C	17.0	10.0	36.0	37.0	134
D	*	50.0	20.0	30.0	31
I	*	50.0	18.0	32.0	22
E	50.0	37.5	12.5	00.0	8
F	87.5	00.0	00.0	12.5	8
J	19.0	26.0	33.0	21.0	42
K	*	53.0	41.0	6.0	32
L[b]	35.5	35.5	16.0	13.0	31
H	*	20.0	20.0	60.0	5
G	25.0	00.0	50.0	25.0	4

[a]Asterisks indicate employers who joined the program after or toward the end of the first quarter. For employers who joined in the last month of the first quarter, referrals made in that month are included with their second-quarter referrals.

[b]An in-house alcoholism program for agency L workers was instituted during the period covered in this table.

work forces to a level that would produce large numbers of referrals. As a result, liaison persons were often kept at "arm's length" and not permitted to undertake broad-based educational programs. As suggested earlier, an employer's agreement to participate in EHP did not automatically guarantee a high level of active support to the project. In fact, for a number of employers, the decision to participate was made by high-level management probably in response to pressures exerted by headquarters for all branch offices and installations to join in the corporation's or government's mandate "to do something positive about alcoholism." That such an attitude can result in what are known as "paper programs"—high on promises but low on results—is well known to evaluators of industrial alcoholism programs (von Wiegand 1973).

A final factor which may have contributed to the rate of referrals was the suspicion with which both management and labor initially viewed the clinic and the university's interest in the project. A natural antiuniversity/antiresearch bias is found among management and union leadership at many levels. The fact that federal funds made the provision of clinic services free to the participating managements and labor unions may have raised further doubts about the absence of local authority, control of the information and guarantees of confidentiality, and vague concerns over possible experimental treatments. There is no doubt that the project gained little cooperation from employers in securing needed data. But this may owe as much to the level of resources that they were willing to invest in the project as it might to ambivalence toward research per se. While the early concerns expressed over the research function seemed to dissipate with the parties' actual experience with the clinic, it is conceivable that such factors could have discouraged some referrals, especially of higher-status professional workers.

Contract Language

Because it was an experiment in furthering multiparty cooperation regarding the treatment of problem drinkers in the work place, EHP believed that institutionalization of the referral mechanism could best be achieved through the development of collective bargaining language. Moreover, since the majority of EHP's potential patients were also members of collective bargaining units, and thus protected by labor contract provisions, contract language would be an effective vehicle for specifying the objectives of the parties' alcoholism policies as well as the guidelines for their application. As part of the project's demonstration goal of furthering the development of contract language on alcoholism, the research staff conducted a study of the state of language among EHP participants, as well as that existing nationwide. While the report of this effort has been published elsewhere (Schramm 1977), some of the findings will be summarized here as they relate to the experiences of participating firms and unions.

The development of comprehensive contract language on alcoholism can be thought of as a dynamic process involving four stages. The first is the recognition by both management and union that, as an area of potential conflict between the parties, alcoholism is an important topic for collective bargaining attention. The second stage involves the generation of political support for incorporating language on alcoholism into the collective bargaining agreement. The third stage marks the beginning of actual language. Negotiations usually result in language outlining the rights and responsibilities of problem drinkers. Language reached at this stage may also contain a joint policy statement regarding the parties' posture toward the problem of alcoholism in the work force, of which treatment may or may not be a component. The final stage, marking the development of truly comprehensive language, occurs when medical insurance is extended to cover treatment. This stage, of course, implies that the parties view alcoholism as a health problem for which treatment will be offered.

Table 3-7, which summarizes the state of contract language between participating managements and unions, shows that in the summer of 1974 six contracts included some language on alcoholism, of which only two contained truly comprehensive language. But the full story of the development of language is not suggested by the table. The AFL-CIO—whose locals represented employees of eight EHP companies, and whose Baltimore Council took over EHP after the demonstration period—has supported active union involvement in industrial al-

49

Table 3-7

State of Labor Agreements between Particpating Managements and Unions with Regard to Language on Alcoholism as of August 1974

Company	Date of Contract Presently in Force	Expiration Date	Alcoholism Policy Statement	Treatment Provided by Employer	Job Security Contingent on Treatment	Sick Leave for Alcoholism Treatment	Health and Medical Coverage for Treatment
L	July 21, 1973	July 20, 1973	Yes	Yes	Yes	–	–
J	July 29, 1974	Open	Yes	–	–	–	–
I	July 17, 1974	June 30, 1976	–	Yes	–	–	–
F	March 29, 1974	March 13, 1976	Yes	–	Yes	Yes	Yes
K	(Personnel Policy Statements 14 & 16)	Open	Yes	Yes	Yes	Yes	–
H	December 10, 1973	September 14, 1976	Yes	Yes	Yes	Yes	Yes

coholism programs since the late 1950s. In 1973 the AFL-CIO's Community Services Department prepared model language that affiliates could present in collective bargaining negotiations (AFL-CIO 1973). Since guidelines developed at the national level only become contract language through local efforts, the Baltimore Council and its member locals are actively working toward inclusion of such model language in contracts covering many EHP workers.

It can be seen, therefore, that in developing support for contract language, EHP unions needed little encouragement. The project did, however, play an important role in this process during the demonstration phase by providing a forum in which management and unions could routinely interact in an ongoing cooperative treatment effort.

4 Treatment

In the approach to treatment adopted and in the nature of services provided, the Employee Health Program (EHP) did not differ substantially from other multimodality outpatient programs. However, in designing a treatment regimen for a defined population—employed problem drinkers—EHP diverged from other clinic efforts with respect to the organization of services as well as in its relationship to the community. This chapter outlines the major assumptions upon which treatment was based, the services offered to EHP patients, the EHP treatment plan, and the goals of treatment.

Strategy of Constructive Confrontation and the Disease Model of Alcoholism

A major impetus for the development of alcoholism control programs within the work place is their superior record of treatment success. Companies that have adopted alcoholism programs have reported recovery rates of 50 to 70 percent, with an average success rate of 66 percent for industry nationwide (von Wiegand 1972). By contrast, a review of twenty-two evaluative studies of alcoholism treatment in nonwork settings reveals success rates ranging from 4 to 75 percent, with the majority of programs (interquartile range) averaging 18 to 35 percent (Mandell 1971).

While such comparisons must be viewed with caution, a key factor in the apparent success of company programs is that referred clients are employed, by definition, and have been found to have had many years of service with their employers. Indeed, a variety of prognostic studies involving alcoholic clients of noncompany treatment centers have identified current employment and job stability as predictors of treatment success (Kissin et al. 1968; Kurland 1968; Trice et al. 1969). It has been argued that a socially stable alcoholic, for example, employed, married, having children, and owning a home, is an excellent candidate for treatment because of his stake in recovery to protect his social wealth. Hence the employed alcoholic who is referred for treatment via a company identification program not only has a social stake (his job) but is also confronted with the threat of losing it unless he takes corrective action.

The value of constructive confrontation has been examined in reports of its use in both noncompany and company programs, and experience has shown that such "nonvoluntary" referral to treatment is not necessarily an obstacle to

51

treatment participation and success (Schramm and DeFillippi 1975). In reviewing a wide range of company programs, Trice and Roman (1972) found that the results of rehabilitation efforts using the confrontation strategy "appear to be better than those of efforts under other conditions." Because of its demonstrated success in industrial alcoholism programs, EHP adopted the tactic of constructive confrontation as the preferred method for identification and referral of problem-drinking employees to the program, and attempted to educate participating managements and unions in its use.

While identifying and referring problem-drinking workers on the basis of unsatisfactory work performance was an important factor in the companies' decision to join the program, equally vital was their belief that alcoholism is primarily a health problem and not a defect in character. This view of alcoholism is compatible with employer support of treatment of retain afflicted workers in the hope of restoring them to past levels of productivity, and with union efforts to bargain for alcoholism treatment as an extension of existing health benefits for their membership. Additionally, by offering medical diagnostic and follow-up services to referred workers, EHP projected an image of professionalism and high-quality care, which was helpful not only in attracting participants to the program but also in securing third-party reimbursement for clinic services.

In planning EHP, the project formulators were aware of the considerable controversy among researchers and clinicians concerning the "disease model" of alcoholism,[1] but adopted the disease concept not only because of its usefulness in educating employers but for therapeutic reasons as well. Other models, while soundly argued in the literature, are only recently being translated into workable plans for treatment. The adoption of the disease model was also justified by the patients themselves, as will be seen in the discussion of the drinking histories of the survey population in chapter 5. EHP counselors estimated that more than three-quarters of the workers referred to the clinic were in relatively advanced stages of alcoholism, and evinced a pattern of drinking that resembled addiction. Indeed, for the 206 workers making up the study population, the percentage of workers who feel into this category was even higher, due to the apparent tendency of the companies to refer the most highly visible problem drinkers first. While the above is in no way meant to suggest that EHP patients are representative of all problem-drinking workers, it does serve to explain the general emphasis of the discussion of treatment in the present chapter.

An Outpatient, Multimodality Approach

The decision to operate EHP as an outpatient facility was influenced by a number of factors. The first is the cost of delivery. The average cost of a full regimen of treatment in an outpatient setting makes it among the least expensive approaches to treatment (see table 4-1). As discussed in chapter 2, cost constraint was an important consideration in ensuring future sponsorship of the

Table 4-1
Cost Comparison of Various Modalities of Treatment[a]

Modality/Facility	Cost per Day
Inpatient treatment	
General Hospital	$95
Specialty Hospital	54
Alcoholism Treatment Center	96
Community Mental Health Center	67-76
Transitional treatment	
Alcoholism Treatment Center	44
Community Mental Health Center	48
Outpatient treatment	
General Hospital	18
Alcoholism Treatment Center	40
Community Mental Health Center	56

[a](From Hallan 1973)

clinic after the demonstration phase. Cost was also a factor for the individual worker. While most EHP patients did have limited coverage for inpatient or residential care, outpatient treatment was wholly compatible with continuous employment. Second, by not taking him out of his home, community, and work role as alternative treatment approaches must, outpatient treatment is uniquely able to build, educate, and utilize the social support network surrounding the patient as part of his extended clinical experience. Finally, outpatient treatment reduces the stigmatization which may be attached to institutionalization by the worker and those around him.

Although there have been numerous attempts to evaluate alcoholism treatment approaches, differences in overall research design as well as in specific criteria used to measure improvements make it impossible to determine the efficacy of outpatient treatment relative to that of inpatient or transitional care (Pattison 1966). Similarly, no specific component of treatment, for example, psychotherapy, drug treatment, group therapy, and behavior modification, can be judged to be superior to another. Investigators have, however, determined the importance of making a wide range of treatment methods and settings available to the patient (Plaut 1967). Thus, the multimodality approach to alcoholism treatment is gaining increasing prominence with the recognition that problem drinking poses a multiplicity of physical, emotional, and social problems. Accordingly, EHP offered to all referred workers medical and psychiatric diagnostic services, individual counseling, group therapy, chemotherapy, and several other counseling and rehabilitative approaches. The range of services made available to EHP workers is summarized in table 4-2.

Table 4–2
Services Available to Patients Referred to EHP

Diagnostic

Complete history, including psychiatric interview
Complete physical examination
Special procedures
    Sigmoidoscopy (as indicated)
    Tonometry (as indicated)
    Endoscopic (as indicated)
Laboratory
    Liver function tests (as indicated
    Pancreatic function tests (as indicated)
    Hematologic tests (as indicated)
    EKG (as indicated)
    Urinalysis (as indicated)
    Chest x-ray (as indicated)
    FMA 12 (as indicated)

Treatment

    Detoxification (as indicated)
    Individual counseling to patient and family
    Group counseling with the patients and their families
    Vocational counseling
    Physical rehabilitation
    Ambulatory medication

Referral

    To other social or therapeutic organizations where applicable (e.g., legal services; specialized examination or treatment; residential program; family physician or psychiatrist; AA or other counseling program)

Follow-up

    History and physical examination
    Special procedures (above, as indicated)
    Laboratory (above, as indicated)
    Counseling
    Physical rehabilitation
    Ambulatory medication
    Referral

Treatment Plan

Treatment was initiated with a prearranged appointment with the clinic's head counselor made by the referring officer in the firm, agency, or union from which the employee was coming. In the case of self-referrals, the "walk-in" approach to treatment was most typical and the head counselor always rearranged time to see a new self-referred patient. The purpose of the initial interview was always the same. The worker-patient was asked about what was causing his problem at work. If it appeared that alcoholism was a major factor, the discussion was directed toward its role in disrupting his life. Since many patients can be expected to deny the extent of their problem with alcohol, the first visit was a low-keyed explanation of what would go on in the course of treatment, and an appointment was made for the patient to return to the clinic to begin treatment. Finally, the rights and responsibilities of EHP patients were explained to the worker, and the initial conference ended with the patient signing a medical release form which outlined all aspects of the expected treatment routine, an employer-data release form which permitted the research group to request data on the patient from his employer, and, for those EHP referrals making up the study population, a statement of consent to participate in the research project by submitting to the intake questionnaire.

During the first month of treatment, the clinical routine was very intensive. On the patient's second visit, both an in-depth discussion with the head counselor and a complete physical examination and tests of physiological functions were conducted. On the third visit, the patient was told of his diagnosis by the physician, including alcoholism where appropriate. For the approximately 25 percent of patients who were diagnosed as having significant unrecognized and untreated ailments, referrals were made to the patient's private physician or an appropriate health service for correction of the condition. As well as demonstrating a level of professionalism and concern for the total patient not usually found in alcoholism programs, the physical diagnosis often confronted the patient with the considerable damage and great life risk that his use of alcohol was producing, and communicated the illness nature of his condition.

About 10 percent of EHP patients were referred for a psychiatric evaluation when the presence of a psychiatric illness in addition to alcoholism was suspected. Occasionally, the neurosis or psychosis was so invasive of all spheres of functioning that the individual was referred for treatment of this primary condition. However, in most cases where both conditions existed, the alcoholism was treated as the primary condition in the belief that as long as the addiction continued, alcohol use would prevent attempts to investigate and treat the other condition. In about 1 percent of all cases referred to EHP, the individual was found to be suffering from neurological or psychiatric illness which resembles alcoholism. Such cases were referred to other treatment programs.

Each patient was assigned to one counselor who was responsible for coordinating the medical and psychiatric appointments, overseeing the patient's progress, tracking down the patient when he failed to appear at the clinic, and developing the patient's individual counseling therapy. During the first month of treatment, the patient met with his counselor about eight times, and in subsequent months at least once every two weeks. In cases where little progress was being made, more frequent meetings were arranged. In addition to individual counseling sessions, a weekly meeting with a group of fellow EHP patients was required of most patients to bring them into contact with other individuals undergoing the same treatment process. Additionally, the patient's counselor arranged for and supervised other treatment modalities as required, including disulfiram therapy, vocational counseling and family counseling or therapy.

For approximately 10 percent of EHP patients, inpatient detoxification or residential treatment was required to restore the patient to a physical or emotional condition appropriate to begin outpatient treatment. About 5 percent of workers arrived at EHP in a life-endangering condition. Withdrawal from alcohol for an individual who has developed physiologic tolerance is potentially dangerous, and should take place under circumstances in which the individual can be observed and put on a regimen of appropriate medication. The counseling staff was prepared to recognize early signs of withdrawal and to transport patients to hospital emergency rooms for immediate care. EHP staff physicians had arrangements with two hospitals for admission of patients for detoxification.

Following an acute toxic condition and detoxification, or for patients whose continual drinking had left them unusually disoriented or depressed, a protected environment was often required in which twenty-four-hour professional and social support could be provided to reconstruct normal life routines and physical help. About 10 percent of EHP patients were referred to private hospitals, specialized alcoholism, residential care facilities, or state hospital alcoholism recovery units for such care. An important advantage of such treatment is that it relieves stress on the family and employer as well as the patient and thereby prevents a precipitous decision made under crisis conditions. EHP maintained contact with the patient through the personnel responsible for treatment in these inpatient facilities so that a plan for continuing treatment after release could be developed.

Finally, three points regarding the treatment environment should be made. Treatment was carried out in surroundings which were designed to be non-threatening and which would approximate the surroundings of a private physician's office. Second, the clinic hours were arranged to accommodate all patients. Because of swing-shift work, early morning and evening hours were necessary. Third, all patient visits were scheduled in advance through the use of appointments. This arrangement was necessary for planning clinic manpower in meeting the requirements of thirteen clinic hours each day, as well as reinforcing the regularity of clinic attendance for the patient.

The EHP treatment sequence was originally envisioned as lasting twelve months, after which time the patient would be discharged from EHP and, where appropriate, referred to a maintenance program, such as a company program (e.g., the U.S. Post Office's PAR program) or AA. Experience showed, however, that few patients opted for discharge after a year. Thus, as of February 15, 1976, of sixty-seven patients in the study population who had been referred to EHP in February 1975 or earlier and who had not dropped out of treatment, fifty-four (81 percent) were still active in the program. Of the thirteen who received discharges from EHP, six were referred to other programs for continued counseling.

Goals of Treatment

Because treatment is a social process involving numerous interpersonal dynamics and interchanges, it is impossible to isolate a particular part of the treatment process as being more important than another. Indeed, since each individual's treatment plan was tailored for him, no single common routine is identifiable as the "core" of the process. What was constant for each patient, however, was the long-term goal of rebuilding the competencies and life-style that would enable him to obtain satisfaction and fulfillment without alcohol. EHP sought to accomplish this by working with the alcoholic or problem drinker through several parallel stages or activities coordinated by his counselor.

The first stage consisted of assembling and verifying the evidence from the worker's own history of the problems that alcohol was causing him, as seen both through his eyes and the eyes of others around him. As mentioned above, one function of the physical examination was to demonstrate to the worker the threat that his continuing use of alcohol posed to his health. Physicians working with the project were instructed to make the connection as dramatic as possible, since the impact of failing health and the prospect of a greatly reduced life span might help to shake the patient out of the self-deception he might have regarding his problem. The circumstances surrounding his coming to EHP, that is, referral by one or more authorities at his job who had observed his declining work performance or attendance, were usually sufficient proof to the patient that his work was suffering and that his very power to earn a living might be in jeopardy if he continued his present drinking behavior. For many EHP workers, the use of alcohol had already contributed to the loss of their families (36 percent of the study population were divorced or separated from their wives) or was presenting considerable domestic difficulties. Additionally, a number of workers had experienced problems with the police and the courts, either having had their licenses revoked for drunk driving or having been arrested for disorderly conduct while intoxicated.

It is important to note that many workers came to EHP already recognizing that alcohol was a serious problem for them. A considerable number had made one or more past attempts to quit drinking on their own, through AA, or in other treatment facilities. Although inappropriate or ineffective forms of treatment may have been responsible for past failures, for most patients previous efforts had consisted of unsuccessful attempts to learn to control their intake in the hope of returning to normal drinking. For such patients, treatment began at the second stage which involved helping the alcoholic to discover that unlike most other drinkers, he cannot control the effects that alcohol has on him.

Most adults in the United States can control the amount of alcohol they use and thus ward off any problematic effects. This is to some extent true in general, but not for the alcoholic. During this stage of treatment the counselor tried to challenge the patient's belief that he was in control of his alcohol use. The challenges often came to a dramatic crescendo when the alcoholic tested his ability to take only a few drinks or to drink without having a decrease in competence. The patient would frequently return surprised, shamefaced, and angry, but conscious that he needed help. But often, the anguish that he experienced over his failure to pass such a test was so great that he could not tolerate exposing it, despairing that he would never be able to effect a change in his drinking. At times such as this, the group therapy was valuable in showing the alcoholic that his problem was not unique and that it could be overcome. In providing the social setting for interpatient reinforcement, the group therapy sessions sought to capture one of the most effective parts of the Alcoholics Anonymous groups. In fact, several groups that operated in the clinic were formally recognized as AA groups; they were run by counselors who were members, and the patient could become an AA member, following the twelve-step AA guide to sobriety (Maxwell 1967).

To some extent, most alcoholics harbor the fantasy that once through the present difficult period, they will be able to resume normal drinking. While necessary throughout the treatment cycle, the support available to the worker from family, friends, supervisors, and union representatives was especially critical during the second phase of treatment when the patient had to become convinced that he would never be able to drink like most other persons. Often, at the initiation of treatment these potential sources of support were at best ambivalent about trying to provide further help. In other cases, coworkers and family would often try to soften the impact of treatment by encouraging the patient to believe that he could eventually "return to normal." Understanding these various reactions, the EHP staff encouraged the expression of ambivalent feelings to lower the level of tension and attempted to mobilize the significant others in the patient's life into supporting his recovery.

The third stage of treatment began when the patient had resolved permanently to reduce or eliminate his use of alcohol. At this point, about 30 percent of EHP patients felt that a medication would help them. A physician prescribed disulfiram (Antabuse) if there were no contraindications. This medication helps patients to avoid taking a drink impulsively by making the ingestion of alcohol the precipitant of violent nausea and other physiological discomforts. Studies have found that the use of disulfiram therapy is an effective part of alcoholism treatment if the patient approaches it as a day-to-day aid to avoid the resumption of drinking (Baekeland et al. 1971; Lundwall and Baekeland 1971). Whether the patient is under medication or not, however, rehabilitation involves a series of life-style changes that extend far beyond giving up alcohol. Since Antabuse can serve as a crutch against facing the necessity for undergoing such change, EHP counselors generally discouraged patients from using it for more than ninety days.

During the third stage of treatment, efforts were focused on helping the worker to create and practice behaviors, interpersonal relationships, and life-style coping patterns to balance the stresses which had been the precipitants for his use of alcohol. Accordingly, the critical counseling task became one of reinforcing the patient's search for accurate and complete information about what was distressing him and the alternatives available, since the alcoholic needs help in keeping stresses in life to a level which he can handle. Here, participating in groups with other alcoholics who were going through similar life changes was often helpful, as was family counseling.

Family counseling methods are a relatively new component of alcoholism treatment programs, and are considered among the most notable advances in the field (Esser 1970; Corder et al. 1972). Since families often adapt themselves around the problem drinking of a household member, families need help in developing new living styles after an alcoholic member ceases drinking. Indeed, tensions may intensify as other problems do not immediately disappear or even worsen after drinking stops (U.S. Department of Health, Education and Welfare 1974). In a number of cases, other members of the worker's family were brought into treatment for their own alcoholism problems as well as for counseling, regarding the most beneficial role which they might play in the recovery of the patient.

Finally, referral of the patient to other community resources was frequently required. Stresses caused by social problems, legal difficulties, and issues involving children could often be mitigated by agencies devoted to these purposes in the community.

Parallel to stress reduction is the problem of increasing life satisfactions. Many alcoholics have been dependent on alcohol and the drinking setting for friendship, conviviality, sexual expression, and a feeling of enhanced competency. By offering sympathetic but firm support and understanding of the worker in trying to overcome his problems, EHP strove to meet some of the dependency needs that had previously been satisfied through his use of alcohol. Avoiding alcohol as well as situations in which it is used, many workers found themselves with large amounts of uncommitted time. Early in treatment, the group meetings filled some of this time. Additionally, the patient often had to relearn social and work skills. This may involve participating in church, union, to civic activities, or enrolling in skill development programs. Finally, while the worker needed help in exploring alternatives, he also had to be aided in accepting the realities of his situation when change was not feasible.

Relapses to drinking may occur at any stage of treatment as frustrations mount. The alcoholic is particularly vulnerable when having achieved sobriety, he discovers how difficult are the changes toward which he must work. In fact, fellow workers and supervisors may have developed expectations over the years that the worker would relapse, and these could have reinforced a return to drinking. Perhaps the most important contribution of the EHP staff was maintaining an attitude of hopefulness about recovery despite relapse. They communicated this hope to the worker, management, and union by their continuing expression of concern for each patient. Additionally, EHP legitimized a definite if not dramatic change in the worker's drinking behavior, conveying a clear announcement under medical authority that had been supported by union and management that the worker was receiving help for reasons of health, not because he was incompetent or immoral. As management and union began to see successes of alcoholic workers who had been referred to EHP, each group to believe that recovery was possible, and EHP participation became associated with hope, a critical element in producing change.

Treatment at EHP was terminated in a series of steps. These included review of various adjustment areas which were sources of frustration at initiation of treatment to ensure that a functioning new source of satisfaction was in place. The patient decreased contract with EHP in stages, as the staff made sure that other supportive relationships were operating. Finally, the patient was encouraged to return at six-month and yearly intervals to review his progress and to be visually reminded of where he was and where others still were. As mentioned above, the worker was encouraged to avail himself of continuing counseling in the form of AA or other treatment agencies.

Modifications to the Treatment Plan

It is important to point out that the discussion in this chapter has been restricted to a presentation of the general approach to treatment. As was indicated above, the therapeutic regimen for any given patient was developed around his individual situation and needs, and thus the treatment approaches and goals outlined here were often modified in individual cases. For example, some patients had no families who could be brought into the treatment and recovery process. Additionally, for some patients the goal of total abstinence was unrealistic. In such cases, attempts were made to assist the patient in altering his pattern and quantity of consumption to minimize impairment and drinking-associated problems to the greatest extent possible.

Similarly, by stressing the ideal model experience of treatment, this chapter has not considered the extent to which this ideal corresponded to the actual treatment experience of the study population. For example, not all patients were referred via constructive confrontation; some referred themselves. Because the intake questionnaire included a series of questions designed to shed some light on issues surrounding the treatment process, chapter 7 will provide additional insights into the treatment experience that bear on the points raised in this chapter. Also, because the primary goal of treatment was to retain problem drinkers on the job, chapter 7 will present the preliminary findings on the employment status of the study population after treatment.

5

Description of the Study Population

This chapter, which begins the presentation of findings from the intake questionnaire, is devoted to a description of the study population. First, data on the drinking and treatment history of the Employee Health Program (EHP) workers are summarized, and their attitudes toward the referral are described. Sociodemographic characteristics of the population are then considered, and the features of EHP referrals' work environment are discussed. Finally, the social stability of the study population is considered with respect to marital status, employment stability, and residential stability. Where data are available, the characteristics of EHP workers are compared with those of other populations of nonskid-row alcoholics.

Drinking History and Attitudes toward
Referral and Treatment

Reports of industrial alcoholism programs have found that, as a rule, workers are not referred for treatment until their problem has progressed to the middle or late stages of alcoholism (Trice 1965). Because EHP served as the first alcoholism identification and referral program for most of the participating employers, it is not surprising that the majority of the study population were found to have had a long history of heavy drinking and of problems associated with excessive consumption of alcohol. As shown in table 5-1, 65 percent of the study population reported that they had been drinking heavily for ten or more years prior to coming to EHP. About one-fifth of the workers began drinking heavily after their twenties, of whom about half had been drinking heavily for more than ten years, and half for less than ten years. The majority of workers in this latter group had previously been drug users and switched to alcohol, thus trading one dependency for another. For almost 70 percent of the study population, however, heavy drinking had begun in the teens or twenties, and continued ever since.

Fifty-seven percent of EHP workers had experienced at least one instance of alcoholism treatment or counseling prior to referral to EHP. Ten percent had had alcoholism treatment other than Alcoholics Anonymous (AA), 26 percent had had such treatment in addition to AA, and 21 percent had been exposed to AA but had had no other form of treatment. This percentage of workers having had previous treatment for alcoholism compares with Smart's population (1974) of company-referred alcoholics, 51.5 percent of whom reported having received prior treatment.

61

Table 5-1
Age Started to Drink Heavily by Years of Heavy Drinking, in Percent

Age Started Heavy Drinking	Years of Heavy Drinking				
	<5	5-9	10-19	20+	Total
<21	2	6	20	21	49
21-29	10	7	6	9	32
30-39	3	1	3	4	11
40-54	5	1	2	0	8
Total	20	15	31	34	100

Also relevant with respect to drinking history are the drinking practices of respondents' families and acquaintances. In their national survey of American drinking practices (ADP Survey) Cahalan et al. (1969) found some significant associations between respondents' drinking practices and the drinking habits of their parents and spouses. For example, 33 percent of all ADP respondents who had fathers who drank frequently (three or more times per week) were heavy drinkers, whereas only 12 percent whose fathers rarely or never drank were heavy drinkers. A similar but even stronger association was found for respondents' mothers and wives.

Table 5-2 shows the EHP respondents' perceptions of the drinking practices of their families while growing up and at the present time, as well as their perceptions of the drinking behavior of their friends and coworkers. While 28 percent of the EHP respondents reported that their fathers drank frequently or constantly while they were growing up, only 5 percent reported having had a mother and 2 percent reporting having had a wife who drank frequently or constantly. These low percentages may be partially attributable to social class. Indeed, Cahalan et al. found a relatively high proportion of abstainers among women married to men working in blue-collar occupations. Also, female abstainers are more frequently found among blacks than whites, and more often in the South than other geographical regions.

But despite the infrequency of drinking among mothers and wives, 33 percent of the study workers felt that at least one person in their home when they were growing up had had a drinking problem, and 17 percent felt a person or persons they now lived with were problem drinkers. Thus, one-third of the study population had family circumstances unfavorable for treatment outcome; investigators have found that positive treatment outcomes are associated with exposure to alcoholism outside the home (Cahalan et al. 1969).

With respect to drinking by friends and coworkers, 67 percent of the respondents said that most of their friends drank frequently or constantly, and 59 percent reported such drinking among their coworkers. Moreover, 72 percent

Table 5–2
Percentage Distribution of EHP Referrals' Perceptions of the Drinking Behavior of their Relatives and Acquaintances

Response	Growing Up				Currently							
	Father	Mother	Sibling	Other	Spouse	Children	Father	Mother	Sibling	Other	Friends	People at Work
Not present	13	6	11	74	49	50	93	90	96	84	–	–
No	24	70	47	9	22	39	2	5	1	5	2	6
Occasionally	34	18	28	6	25	8	3	4	–	8	31	34
Frequently	16	4	10	7	1	2	1	–	1	1	34	36
Constantly	12	1	5	3	1	–	–	–	1	1	33	23

felt that some of their friends were problem drinkers, and 63 percent felt this to be true of their coworkers (Trice et al. 1969).

With the exception of self-referrals, problem-drinking workers were referred to EHP under constructive confrontation, and in that sense were "nonvoluntary referrals." Historically, the position of many alcoholism therapists has been to regard the voluntary seeking of treatment as an indicator of patient motivation and, hence, of treatment success (Sterne and Pittman 1965). Twenty-six patients (13 percent of the population) came to EHP entirely on their own volition, that is, not under threat of job loss, and thus could be considered to be highly motivated. However, responses of the remaining 87 percent to questions regarding their attitudes toward referral and treatment indicated that the majority of these patients expressed a favorable disposition to treatment. Eighty percent felt that the referral was appropriate and 76 percent felt that they had a drinking problem serious enough to warrant treatment. Only 15 percent thought that the referral was inappropriate, and 5 percent were uncertain. Similarly, just 18 percent saw no need for treatment, with 6 percent being uncertain. Taking both questions together, only 23 percent expressed negative or ambivalent feelings toward the referral, the need for treatment, or both. Thus, the attitudes of EHP workers at intake support the findings of other studies that nonvoluntary referral is not necessarily a barrier to a patient's acceptance of treatment (see chapter 4).

Sociodemographic Characteristics

Age

The age distribution of the study population was twenty to twenty-nine (12 percent), thirty to thirty-nine (23 percent), forty to forty-nine (41 percent), and fifty to sixty-four (24 percent). The median age of referred workers was 43.2 (mean = 42.5; mode = 41). This median age is similar to that found in other treatment populations of employed alcoholics (Straus and Bacon 1951; Smart 1974), with the majority of workers (58 percent) falling within the thirty-five to fifty age group as expected (Trice 1959).

Race

The racial distribution of the study population was 61 percent black and 39 percent white, whereas in the Baltimore male labor force, the percentages are exactly the reverse. This racial composition distinguishes the EHP study population from all other reports of problem drinkers in their work roles, and, consequently, in analyzing the EHP data, special attention was given to determining whether there were any significant differences between blacks and whites in socioeconomic and work characteristics and in responses to treatment.

In a review of the literature on black drinking practices, Sterne and Pittman (1972) found that even in studies unbiased by who seeks or is accepted for treatment or who is apprehended for alcohol-associated offenses, "Negro alcoholism and problem drinking rates often range from one and a half to four times higher than White rates." The authors go on to qualify, however, stating that "Race differentials may reflect in part the gross nature of comparisons when Negroes are compared to 'Whites' in general, rather than to other persons who occupy a similar position in the structure of American society."

That this latter statement may best characterize the meaning of racial differences in drinking and alcoholism is supported by multivariate analyses of treatment outcomes that find racial differences all but disappearing when social-class variables are taken into account (Kissin et al. 1968). Indeed, much of the explanation for the disproportionately high percentage of blacks in the EHP study population may lie in their concentration in low-status jobs, as will be shown below.

Occupation

Table 5-3 shows that for EHP referrals, as for the Baltimore work force as a whole, the proportion of blacks in each occupational grouping increases as occupational status decreases. However, as expected on the basis of previous studies of company-identified treatment populations, which consistently find an overrepresentation of low-skill-level workers (Trice 1965*a*; Warkov et al. 1965), table 5-4 shows that both blacks and whites in the study population occupied fewer higher-status positions and more lower-status positions than their counterparts in the Baltimore labor force.[1]

Since we do not have data on the occupational distributions of the referring companies' labor forces, or a record of workers who were identified and referred elsewhere, we do not know the precise magnitude of the selective bias toward identification of lower-status workers to EHP. There is good reason to believe, however, that in the EHP population white-collar workers are even more underrepresented and unskilled blue-collar workers more overrepresented relative to the population at risk than indicated in table 5-4. As shown in table 5-5, industrial employers referred almost no white-collar workers to EHP, and among the blue-collar subgroupings, the percentage of referrals increases with decreasing job status. With respect to referrals by government service agencies, employing primarily white-collar workers, low-status laborers and service workers would also appear to be considerably overrepresented.

Education, Religion, and Place of Birth

The median number of years of formal schooling completed by EHP referrals was ten. Fifty percent of the study population had completed fewer than twelve years of education, of whom slightly more than half had never attended high school. Of those who completed high school (35 percent of the population), 28 percent earned a high school equivalency after having dropped out of school. Not surprisingly, the level of education completed reflected occupational position.

Table 5-3
Race by Occupation, in Percent

	Professionals/ Managers	Clerical Sales	Craftsmen	Operatives	Service Workers	Laborers	Total
EHP study population							
Black	27	41	46	72	70	78	61
White	73	59	54	28	30	22	39
							100
Baltimore City Employed Male Work Force[a]							
Black	19	28	32	53	56	71	39
White	81	72	68	47	44	29	61
							100

[a](U.S. Bureau of the Census 1972)

Table 5–4
Occupation by Race, in Percent

Occupation	EPH Study Population			Baltimore City Male Work Force		
	Black	White	Total	Black	White	Total
Professionals/ Managers	3	14	7	9	26	19
Clerical/sales	9	20	13	11	19	16
Craftsmen	13	25	19	17	25	22
Operatives	30	19	26	31	18	23
Service workers	11	8	10	16	4	11
Laborers	33	15	26	15	8	10
Total	99	101	101	99	100	101

Table 5–5
Percentage Distribution of Occupations of Referred Workers by Type of Employer

EHP Study Population		Industrial Employers (68% of Referrals)	Government Service Employers[a] (32% of Referrals)
White Collar		1.5	56
Blue collar	Skilled	27.0	7
	Semiskilled	34.0	2
	Unskilled	37.5	35
		100.0	100

[a]Excludes the city sanitation department which is known to have a predominantly low-skilled blue-collar work force.

Professional and clerical workers accounted for 92 percent of the workers (15 percent of the population) who had had one or more years of college.

Twenty-four percent of EHP referrals practiced no religion, 64 percent were Protestants, and 16 percent Catholics. Those who practiced no religion were found disproportionately among the twenty-one to twenty-nine age group and among whites. Seventy-five percent of black EHP workers were Protestants.

With the exception of one individual, the study workers were all native-born citizens, and the great majority (95 percent) were long-term residents (eight or more years) of Maryland. Forty-nine percent were born in Maryland, 42 percent in the South, and 9 percent in other regions of the country.

Income

The U.S. Department of Labor's Bureau of Labor Statistics has estimated the annual consumption budget for a family of three (husband and wife aged thirty-five to fifty-four with one child) to be $6000 at the lower level, $8920 at the intermediate level, and $12,280 at the higher level.[2] In the month preceding intake, 36 percent of the study population reported a combined household income of $500 to $833, and 54 percent reported an income of $834 or higher. Eleven percent had a combined income of less than $500, suggesting an annual income below $6000. It is important to note, however, that not all respondents worked a full month in the period under question. In fact, of the thirty-nine workers who reported earning less than $500 in the month prior to interview, twenty-nine had been on disciplinary suspension or sick leave at least part of the time. Of the remaining ten, seven were service workers and three were laborers whose yearly salary was less than $6000.

Current Employment Experience

It has already been established that workers referred to EHP comprised a population of primarily low-status, blue-collar workers in a heavy industrial setting. To provide a clearer picture of the work experiences of referred workers, this section will describe the jobs held by the study population with respect to the range of occupations represented within the major census groupings, the level of training the workers received for their jobs, and several features of the work environment.

Occupations

Only fifteen workers (7 percent of the study population) held professionals or managerial jobs. These fell into three groupings: engineers (six), computer programmers and data analysts (six), and state correctional or rehabilitation officers (three). Of the twenty-seven clerical workers (13 percent of the population), there were eight clerks, seven letter carriers, seven office machine or computer operators, and five dispatchers.

Eighty percent of the population (164 workers) were blue-collar workers and service workers. Within the census category of craftsmen/foremen were thirty-seven of the referred workers, representing seven occupations: crane operators (nine), electricians (eight), mechanics (seven), foremen (five), shipfitters (four), cable installers (two), and bricklayers (two). Within the operative category were fifty-three workers, the majority of whom (thirty-five) were steelworkers. The occupations held by the fifth-three operatives were mechanical helpers (twelve), machine operators (eleven), heavy-equipment (e.g., bulldozer) operators (nine), furnace attendants (seven), truck drivers (four), welders (three), assembly-line workers (three), and miscellaneous steelworkers (four).

The remaining 36 percent of the population worked in the categories of unskilled labor (fifty-four) and service (twenty). About four-fifths of the laborers (forty-two) worked in heavy industries, half of whom were nonassigned pool laborers, working as needed, primarily for loading or unloading and heavy-duty clean-up detail, and half of whom were assigned to specific duties, for example, furnace and shipbuilding laborers. Eight laborers worked for the state or city governments as sanitation workers or groundkeepers, and four were post office laborers, that is, mail handlers. The majority of service workers (fourteen) were janitors/custodians, and of the remaining six, three were health services and three were child care workers. Table 5-6 lists the occupations of the study workers within each census classification.

Skill Level

Given the predominance of unskilled and semiskilled blue-collar workers, it is not surprising that only 17 percent of the population reported having received formal training for their present jobs. Table 5-7 shows the training received by EHP workers according to occupational level. Forty-four percent reported receiving no training at all, including a surprising number of craftsmen and operatives, suggesting that many workers attained these positions on the basis of seniority. Thus, laborers may be promoted to the operative position of bull-dozer operator, and a bulldozer operator may become a crane operator (classified

Table 5-6
Occupations Held by the Study Population

Occupations	N	Occupations	N
Professionals/managers		*Operatives*	
Engineers	6	Assembly-line workers	3
Computer programmers	6	Furnace attendants	7
Correctional/rehabilitation officers	3	Heavy-equipment operators	9
Managers	—	Machine operators	11
Personnel specialists	—	Mechanical helpers	12
	15	Other steelworkers	4
		Truck drivers	4
Clerical workers		Welders	3
Clerks	8		53
Dispatchers	5		
Letter carriers	7	*Laborers*	
Office machine or computer operators	7	Assigned laborers	21
	27	Mail handlers	4
		Nonassigned laborers	21
Craftsmen/foremen		Sanitation workers	8
Bricklayers	2		54
Cable installers	2		
Carpenter	—	*Service workers*	
Crane operators	9	Child care workers	3
Electricians	8	Custodians/janitors	14
Foremen	5	Health service workers	3
Mechanics	7		20
Shipfitters	4		
	37		

Table 5-7
Training Received by Study Population for Present Job
(in percent)

Training Received for Present Job	Professionals/Managers	Clerical/Sales	Craftsmen	Operatives	Service Workers	Laborers	Total N	Total %
				Occupation				
No training of any kind	6	20	25	46	63	70	(80)	44
On-the-job training only	20	72	41	44	21	30	(71)	39
Training other than on the job	74	8	34	10	16	—	(31)	17
Total	100	100	100	100	100	100	(182)	100

as a craftsman's occupation), with perfunctory on-the-job training or no training at all, having observed these functions being performed on a day-to-day basis over a number of years. Indeed, only a third of the workers classified as craftsmen can be said to conform to the image of highly skilled laborers in the sense of having completed a formal period of apprenticeship training.

To obtain some notion of the company's investment in the worker, respondents who had received formal training were asked whether it had been paid for by the company. Of the thirty-one workers who had received such training, were thirteen whose employers had paid for it: six professionals, two clerical workers, two craftsmen, and three child care (service) workers. Thus, the image of alcoholic workers as highly skilled employees in whom the firm has a considerable investment does not quite apply to the study population. While it is true that alcoholism most often affects workers in the productive years of age thirty-five to fifty, within that age group, as within any other, are workers having a mix of skills, ranging from those that are highly specialized and difficult to replace to those that are more diffuse and whose precise contribution to the firm are much more difficult to assess. Moreover, given the highly interdependent nature not only of industrial production but also of many clerical functions, it can be argued that positions most nearly approximating the former image are held by only a minority of workers within any given labor force.

Features of the Work Environment

In describing the job experiences of workers most often singled out for referral to company alcoholism programs, Trice and Roman (1972) note that identification of workers tends to vary in relationship to the interdependence and visibility of their task functions. This is a major explanation for the predominance of blue-collar low-status workers in company treatment populations. Not surprisingly, then, when EHP workers were asked to describe their jobs in terms of six aspects of their work and task environments, the responses, summarized in table 5-8, yielded a picture of workers performing highly defined tasks dependent upon supervision and interdependent with the work of others. More than eighty percent of the respondents worked in departments of twenty or more workers and performed their jobs in cooperation with others, and over ninety percent worked a fixed time schedule, with no supervisory role and no ambiguity regarding what was required of them.

Social Stability

Investigators often use scales composed of marital, employment, and residential characteristics to describe the social stability of treatment populations (Straus and Bacon 1951; Gerard and Saenger 1966; Kurland 1968).

Table 5-8
Features of the Work Environment

	Study Population, %
Size of department	
1–4	4
5–19	10
20–49	16
50+	70
	100
Number of people worked with in performing job	
0	17
1–4	32
5–9	21
10+	30
	100
Supervisory function	
Yes	9
No	91
	100
Time schedule	
Flexible	3
Fixed	97
	100
Shift Worked	
Days	55
Noon	9
Nights	6
Swing/rotating	25
When wanted	4
	99
How often knowing what is required on job	
Most times know	91
Sometimes don't know	7
Often don't know	2
	100

Marital Status

Marital status is frequently cited as an important factor associated with drinking patterns and practices, and being married, along with living in a family setting, an indicator of social stability (Gerard and Saenger, 1966). A history of marital disintegration has been found to be common among alcoholics, with the rates of separation, divorce, and widowhood often exceeding considerably those of the population as a whole (Bailey 1961). As shown in table 5-9, the marital status of EHP referrals differed substantially from that of the Baltimore male

Table 5-9
Marital Status

| Marital Status | Study Population | | Baltimore City Male Population |
	n	%	%
Single	22	11	26
Married	101	49	59
Widowed	9	4	5
Divorced	20	10	4
Separated	54	26	6
Totals	206	100	100

population (U.S. Bureau of the Census 1972), especially with respect to divorce and separation.

The percentage of married EHP workers was only somewhat lower than that reported for two other populations of employed alcoholics. Straus and Bacon's survey (1951) of 2023 clinic patients found 53 percent to be married, and in Smart's study (1974) of 200 workers referred under a company alcoholism program, 56.5 percent were married. With respect to the number of children and dependents, the survey population had an average of 2.7 children in or out of the home, and an average of 2.4 dependents. The living arrangements of the study population will be considered below in the discussion of residential stability.

There proved to be no dramatic differences in marital status according to race. Eight percent fewer blacks were married and 6 percent more blacks divorced or separated than whites. Fifty-seven percent of white-collar workers were married versus 47 percent of blue-collar workers, but only 4 percent more blue-collar than white-collar workers were divorced or separated, with blue-collar workers having more single and widowed workers.

As noted above, 22 percent of the population had never married, with the majority of these (68 percent) in the twenty to thirty-nine age group, 14 percent were forty to forty-nine, and 18 percent fifty to sixty-four years of age. Despite evidence of past marital disintegration, multiple marriages did not characterize this population. Of the 184 referred workers who were still or had been married, 154 (84 percent) had been married only one time, 27 (15 percent) twice, 1 three times, and 2 five times. Of those presently widowed, divorced, or separated from their wives, almost half (48 percent) had been living away from their spouse for five or more years, and 37 percent from one to five years. Thus, fewer than 5 percent of the study population came to the clinic with very recent (eight months or less) marital disruptions.

Employment Stability

Eighty-eight percent of the study population were still working for the referring employer at the time of interview. As one condition for participating in the project, employers agreed not to terminate workers referred to EHP as long as they were in treatment and regularly attending the clinic. Nevertheless, twenty-four workers (12 percent of the population) were unemployed at the time of interview, for the most part, having been referred by union officials with the expectation that they might be rehired if they could demonstrate improvement in treatment.

Measures of employment stability beyond simply having a job include number of years with one's employer (job tenure) and the frequency of job changing. The median job tenure of EHP workers was ten years, with only 6 percent of the workers having been with their employers for less than one year. Sixty-five percent of the study population had had only one employer, 19 percent two employers, and 15 percent three or more employers in the five years before their referral to the clinic. Hence, consistent with the findings of other surveys of nonskid-row alcoholics (Trice and Roman 1972), labor force instability was not a feature of the EHP population.

While the above finding of labor force stability will be subjected to closer scrutiny in chapter 6, it is important to note here that, although EHP workers had, in general, spent many years working for the same employer, their work performance itself could not be characterized as stable. On the basis of the work history forms supplied by EHP employers on workers after their referral to the clinic (see chapter 1, pp. 6-7), it can be seen that the study population evinced an excessive level of absenteeism. This can come as no surprise to those familiar with the literature on occupational alcoholism, as declining work performance, particularly in the form of excessive hours lost from work (absenteeism and tardiness) is frequently characteristic of problem drinkers (Trice and Roman 1972). Table 5-10 shows the absence experience of the treatment population and the work force at risk of the eleven employers who supplied the relevant information. Although the data are incomplete, it is obvious that absenteeism of EHP workers is much greater than that of the work force at risk. Expressed in terms of potential full work-years lost due to alcohol misuse, assuming a normal work-year of 2000 hours, workers referred to EHP had missed a maximum of 26 percent and a minimum of 8 percent of the work-year prior to referral, whereas all workers at risk in the labor forces of the participating employers lost 6 percent and 2 percent, respectively. Reviewing a number of studies, Trice and Roman (1972) found that the absenteeism rates of alcoholic workers reported ranged from two to eight times those of all employees. Likewise, the absenteeism of EHP referrals, as a factor of that of the work force at risk, exceeded the normal experience by a minimum of 3.8 to a maximum of 8.3 times.

Table 5-10
Average Hours Lost by Treatment Population and Work Force at Risk by Participating Employer, Year Prior to Referral[a]

Employer	Average Hours Lost by Entire Work Force at Risk-Year	Rate (Days)	Average Hours Lost by Referred Treatment Population during Year Prior to Referral n = (129)	Rate	Average Hours Lost by Referred Workers ÷ Average Hours Lost by Population at Risk
C	74.3	0.037	478	0.272	6.4
D	*	*	582	0.332	*
F	*	*	461	0.263	*
B	52.0	0.029	186	0.104	3.5
K	*	*	265	0.150	*
I	128.0	0.072	445	0.254	3.4
E	52.8	0.030	236	0.136	4.5
J	90.4	0.051	510	0.290	5.6
L	64.0	0.036	535	0.314	8.3
A	*	*	165	0.095	*
H	60.8	0.034	328	0.186	5.3

[a]Asterisks indicate data not supplied by employer.

Residential Stability

Once aspect of residential stability concerns the type of dwelling in which an individual lives, with single-room occupancy considered to be negatively associated and home ownership positively associated with treatment outcomes. Of the 206 EHP respondents, 4 percent (eight persons) lived in a single room, 33 percent in apartments, and 64 percent in houses or mobile homes. Thirty-one percent of EHP referrals owned their own homes, compared with 43 percent in Baltimore City.

It can be deduced, therefore, that of the 25 percent of the study population who are living alone, five out of six were living in conventional dwellings. The 21 percent of the study population who were thus living alone as head of household, is not substantially different from Baltimore City where the figure was 25 percent in 1970. The majority of those living alone were divorced, widowed, or separated, whereas never married individuals tended to live in family units. The living situation of those living in households also appeared to be favorable in the sense of little crowding; 68 percent lived in households having two to four persons, and only 9 percent lived in households having seven or more. For the study population as a whole, the mean number of household members was 3.8, compared with 3.07 for Baltimore City in 1970.

As noted earlier, 95 percent of the study population had lived in Maryland for eight or more years at the time of intake. Only one individual had lived in the state for less than a year. Table 5-11 shows changes in residence during the past five years and the number of years at the present address. Thus, 71 percent of the population had been living at the same address for two or more years.

Table 5-11
Number of Years at Present Address and Number of Addresses in Past Five Years

Number of years at present address	Study Population	
	n	%
>8	71	34
5–8	29	14
2–5	47	23
<2	59	29
	206	100
Number of addresses in the past five years		
1	95	46
2	59	29
3–4	38	18
5–7	10	5
8–15	4	2
	206	100

This compares with 66 to 75 percent (the range for four subpopulations) of Smart's company-referred treatment population. However, one-fourth of the EHP population were frequent movers, having had from three to fifteen moves over the five-year period prior to intake.

Social Stability of EHP Workers Compared with That
of Other Treatment Populations

A social stability scale often cited in the literature is Gerard and Saenger's four-point scale (1966) based on the criteria of whether the patient was (1) married, (2) living with his family, and (3) regularly employed at intake. They found 31 percent of their population fulfilling all three criteria, 28 percent scored 2, 23 percent scored 1, and 18 percent (described by the authors as in skid-row or comparable social settings) fulfilled none. In their study of alcoholism and social stability of 2023 male clinic patients, Straus and Bacon (1951) used a five-point scale, using as criteria of positive indexes of stability (1) having held a steady job for at least three years; (2) residential immobility for at least two years; (3) living in either own home or that of relatives or friends; and (4) being married and living with wife. The patients were rated from 4 to 0, depending on the number of these criteria which they displayed, as follows: 30% = 4, 31% = 3, 21% = 2, 12% = 1, and 5% = 0.

Table 5-12 shows the social stability of the study population, using Gerard and Saenger's four-point scale. Forty-three percent of the population satisfied all three criteria, 28.5 percent scored 2, 26 percent scored 1, and only 2.5 percent

Table 5-12
Social Stability of Study Population

Number of Criteria Satisfied	Criteria	n	%
3	Married, living with ones family, and employed	88	43.0
2	Unmarried, living in a family setting, and employed	46	22.5
2	Married, living with ones family, but unemployed	13	6.0
1	Unmarried, living in a family setting, and unemployed	6	3.0
1	Unmarried, living alone, but employed	48	23.0
0	Unmarried, living alone, and unemployed	5	2.5
		206	100.0

satisfied none of the criteria. Ten percent more whites than blacks ranked highest on social stability; however, with respect to relative instability, the difference was much smaller, with 29 percent of blacks and 27 percent of whites scoring 0 or 1. Sixty-five percent of EHP referrals scored 2 to 3, compared with 59 percent of the clients of Gerard and Saengers' eight outpatient clinics. Although the criteria are not identical, the EHP study population, with 65.5 percent scoring 2 to 3 on a four-point scale, would appear to compare favorably with Straus and Bacon's population, of whom 61 percent scored 3 or 4 on a five-point scale. Smart (1974), describing the social stability of his company-referred treatment population, noted only that "most patients fulfilled the maximum criteria as stated by Gerard and Saenger." Given the fact that 90 percent lived in family settings, 98 percent were employed, and 56.5 percent were married, Smart's population would score higher on social stability than the EHP study population, for whom corresponding figures are 75, 88, and 49 percent. Overall, however, the social stability of the EHP study population compares favorably with that found in other populations of non-skid-row alcoholics.

**Comparison of EHP
Study Workers and Their
Nonproblem-Drinking Peers**

As mentioned in chapter 1, the comparison population was drawn not only as a means for comparing selected social and work history characteristics of EHP alcoholics with those of nonalcoholics in the same work force, but also for purposes of understanding the feelings and attitudes of alcoholic workers toward their jobs. Following a brief description of the comparison group, this chapter will examine the similarities and differences between the two populations with respect to social stability, work force behavior, and job and life satisfaction.

The Comparison Population

To establish that they were, in fact, a sample of nonalcoholic, nonproblem-drinking workers, the responses of the comparison group to questions on drinking behavior were examined, using criteria set down by Cahalan et al. (1969) in their survey of normal American drinking practices (ADP). The comparison workers were classified according to the following drinking types: abstainers (20 percent), infrequent drinkers (15 percent), light and moderate drinkers (38 percent), and heavy drinkers (27 percent). The equivalent breakdown for ADP survey male operatives (the modal occupational category of comparison workers) was 27 percent, 12 percent, 35 percent, and 26 percent, respectively (Cahalan et al. 1969). It is reasonable to conclude, therefore, that the drinking behavior of the comparison group was characteristic of that of a normal population of industrial workers. Only two comparison workers reported having had any problems connected with alcohol consumption in the month prior to interview, and none reported having received treatment for alcoholism any time in the past.

As was explained in chapter 1, the data of the 100 male workers forming the comparison group were obtained from telephone interviews of individuals working for EHP participating employers on the basis of their similarity to study workers as regards race, age, occupation, income,[1] and education. Table 6-1 shows that the populations are nearly identical with respect to race and household income in the month preceding intake. The difference in high school completion is accounted for by a greater percentage of comparison than study workers having earned high school equivalency; the median years of formal schooling are identical for both groups. Although the comparison group is somewhat older than the study population, the greatest difference being in the

Table 6-1

Comparison of Survey and Comparison Populations with Respect to Race, Age, Occupation, Education, and Income

	Survey Population, %	Comparison Group, %
Race		
Black	61	60
White	39	40
Age		
20–39	35	31
40–49	41	36
50–64	24	33
Median	(43)	(47)
Occupation		
Professionals/managers	7	8
Clerical/sales	13	12
Craftsmen	19	25
Operatives	26	32
Service workers	10	–
Laborers	26	23
Education		
12	50	43
12	50	57
High school equivalency as % of all high school graduates	28	35
Median years of formal schooling	(10)	(10)
Household income		
<$500	11	10
$500+	89	90

fifty to sixty-four age group, there are sufficient numbers in each category so that age differences can be controlled where necessary. While there was no attempt to match the groups with respect to place of birth, the fact that almost half of the comparison group were born in the South adds another dimension of similarity to the two populations. Additionally, there were not significant differences between the groups with respect to numbers of children and dependents, religion, home ownership, and average number of household members for those not living alone.

The major difference between the populations is that of occupation, with the comparison group having no service workers, and having more craftsmen and operatives and fewer laborers than the study population. Again, with the exception of service workers, there are sufficient numbers in each blue-collar category to permit comparisons on job attitude variables. Moreover, although the comparison group contains a smaller proportion of its workers in the lowest-status blue-collar jobs, the groups proved to be very similar with respect to features of the work environment. As is true of the study population, more than 80 percent of the comparison group worked in departments of twenty or more workers and performed their jobs in cooperation with others, and over 90 percent worked a fixed-time schedule, with no supervisory role and no ambiguity regarding what was required of them.

Social Stability Differences between the Study and Comparison Groups

While the social stability of the study population compared favorably with that of other treatment populations, it will be instructive to see how this stability compares with that of a group of nonproblem-drinking workers drawn from the same labor force. Rather than using Gerard and Saenger's scale of social stability (1966), which emphasizes primarily living situation (two out of three criteria), a modified seven-point scale of social stability was devised, using the criteria listed in table 6-2. As columns 1 and 2 in the table show, the comparison group scored much higher in social stability on all three dimensions measured. Table 6-3 shows the overall stability scores of both groups. Clearly, with 85 percent scoring either 5 or 6, versus only 36 percent for EHP referrals, the comparison group presents a significantly greater picture of social stability than does the treatment population.

Another indicator of social stability is serious trouble with the police. Here too, there were significant differences between study and comparison workers, as shown in table 6-4, which gives the responses of both groups to the question, How many times have you been in jail for any reason? The fact

Table 6-2
Social Stability of Study and Comparison Workers

Study Population, %	Comparison Group, %	Stability Criteria	Number of Points
49	76	Married and living with spouse	2
46	82	One address in past five years	2
65	91	One job in past five years	2
26	17	Single, widowed, divorced or separated and living in a family setting	1
29	17	Two addresses in past five years	1
19	4	Two jobs in past five years	1
25	7	Single, widowed, divorced or separated and living alone	0
25	1	Three or more addresses in past five years	0
16	5	Three or more jobs in past five years, or unemployed at time of intake	0

Table 6-3
Modified Social Stability Scale

| Social Stability Score | EHP Referrals | | Comparison Group |
	n	%	%
6	39	19.0	64
5	35	17.0	21
4	50	24.0	8
3	31	15.0	4
2	34	16.5	3
1	14	7.0	–
0	3	1.5	–
Total	206	100.0	100

$X^2 = 65.813$, d.f. $= 2, p < .005$.

Table 6-4
Times Jailed Any Time in the Past

| | Study Population | | | | Comparison Group | | |
| | Black | White | Total | | Black | White | Total |
Times Jailed	n	n	n	%	%	%	%
9	36	44	(80)	39	69	80	74
1–2	29	31	(62)	30	22	10	17
3–4	16	8	(26)	13	7	10	8
≥5	19	17	(38)	19	2	–	1
	100	100	(206)	100	100	100	100

X^2 (for totals) $= 39.527$, d.f. $= 3, p > .005$.

that these instances of prior jailings include juvenile as well as adult offenses may be at least a partial explanation of why a higher percentage of prior arrests occurred among black than white respondents in both groups. However, the differences between study blacks and whites having had no arrests is only 8 percent, compared with a 19 percent difference among the comparison workers. Ten percent more study blacks than whites had three or more arrests, while only 2 percent more blacks had one or two prior jailings. The high percentage of previous arrests for both blacks and whites in the study population is consistent with findings reported by Kurland (1968). Among white males receiving alcoholism treatment in a state hospital in Baltimore, 90 percent of the patients admitted to at least one previous arrest.

Although the findings reported in this section may appear trivial in the light of many previous studies on the social disruptions produced by alcohol misuse, much of the literature on working alcoholics tends to emphasize their high degree of social stability, often to the point of suggesting that alcoholic employees are even more stable than their nonproblem-drinking counterparts. Such an emphasis seems to be more understandable when it is recalled that the "discovery of working alcoholics" was long delayed by the stereotypic image of alcoholics as primarily skid-row derelicts. Certainly, EHP referrals were far from conforming to such an image. Nevertheless, when compared with their peers of nonproblem drinkers, it would seem clear that alcohol misuse does have an impact on several spheres of normal life functioning.

Work Force Behavior

It has been well-established that the productivity of alcoholic employees is inferior to that of other, nonproblem-drinking workers, with respect to quality of output and absenteeism. But there are many other aspects of work experience that may be adversely affected by alcohol misuse. To extend present knowledge about the work behavior of alcoholics, the intake questionnaire included many items on work experiences, both past and present. In this section, the comparison and study groups are compared with respect to age at labor force entry, number of employers, occupational mobility, and job tenure with current employer.

Work History

Thirteen percent more EHP than comparison workers held their first jobs before age eighteen (X^2 = 6.042, d.f. = 1, $p < 0.025$), even though the median year of formal schooling was the same for both groups. The difference is explained by more EHP than comparison workers having held part-time jobs at an earlier age, suggesting less stable economic and social circumstances in the families of study workers while growing up. In fact, such concomitants of early labor force entry as loss of a parent and financial hardship have led some investigators to argue that entering the labor force at an early age may be a precursor of alcohol dependency (Perry et al. 1970).

Twenty percent of the study population and 39 percent of the comparison group had had only one full-time employer since entering the civilian labor force. Sixty-five percent of EHP and 91 percent of control workers had only one employer in the five years before interview. Thus, more comparison than study workers had spent the better part of their working careers with the employer they were working for at the time of interview, although the tendency to settle into one job perceived as providing a secure future and steady income was characteristic of both populations. Of those who had held previous jobs, 66 percent of study and 64 percent of comparison workers gave more money, job security, or better working conditions as the reason for leaving their previous employers. Only 6 percent of study and 7 percent of comparison workers mentioned work content as a reason for changing jobs.

A British survey of 300 recently employed alcoholics found the majority to have work histories characterized by no occupational advancement, and even by downward mobility (Edwards et al. 1967). For 59 percent of study workers the most recent change in employer involved no change in occupational status; 23 percent moved into a higher occupational status; and 18 percent moved into a lower one.[2] Although these figures suggest little occupational mobility, the experience of comparison workers did not differ significantly (60 percent had no change; 28 percent moved upward and 12 percent, downward).

While the majority of workers in both groups had been working for many years for the same employer and, for the most part, at the same occupational level they held with previous employers, they had not necessarily worked at the same job. Forty-two percent of the study population had continued in the same job they had when first joining the company, but 30 percent reported having had three or more different jobs. However, comparison workers reported more job changes with their present employer, with the number of job changes increasing in direct proportion to years on the job for both groups.

The absence of upward occupational mobility among both groups of workers is consistent with sociological studies of intergenerational mobility, which show that workers evince a strong tendency to hold occupations similar to those of their fathers. While there are shifts from one occupational group to another, especially in the lower strata, these are on the whole shifts to positions of similar status (Lipset and Bendix 1959; Robinson 1969). At the time of interview, 49 percent of study workers and 45 percent of the comparison group were working in occupations similar to those held by their fathers. Thirty-six percent of study and 38 percent of comparison workers held a higher position than their fathers, with the majority of these being skilled or semiskilled blue-collar workers, whose fathers were laborers.

Thus, although EHP referrals had reported many years of heavy drinking and a majority had been treated for alcoholism before being referred to EHP, their work histories showed little evidence of a pattern of downward mobility when viewed against the experience of their nonproblem-drinking counterparts in the same work force.

Job Tenure

Previous investigators have found that frequent job turnover is not a characteristic of alcoholic employees (Trice 1962; Straus and Bacon 1951). Indeed, Warkov and Bacon (1965) found that workers identified as problem drinkers by their supervisors had longer job tenure than their nonproblem-drinking counterparts in the same work force.

The median job tenure of EHP workers was ten years, with 53 percent having worked for the referring employer for ten years or longer. Although the job tenure of EHP workers was longer than that of male workers of similar age in the U.S. labor force (Hayghe 1974), the median job tenure of the comparison workers was twice as long (twenty years) as that of study workers, with 76 percent having been on the same job for ten years or more. Furthermore, 16 percent of EHP workers had been on the job for two years or less, compared with only 2 percent of comparison workers. The differences between the two groups in job tenure ($X^2 = 28.974$, d.f. = 3, $p < .005$) were pronounced, regardless of age, race, or occupaion.

While it might be argued that the sampling procedure used to obtain the comparison group acted to select out workers having atypical longevity, Siassi et al. (1973), using a probability sample of 937 auto workers to survey the drinking practices of United Automobile Workers (UAW) members in Baltimore, found the average number of years at the present job to be 13.5. Since the median age of these UAW members was forty, compared with forty-seven for the control group, a median tenure of twenty years for control workers seems credible. Moreover, information on the job tenure and age of the work forces of the eight participating employers who supplied such data indicates that relatively long job tenure is a characteristic of the population at risk. Table 6-5 shows that for the work forces of participating employers, the median job tenure ranged from 7.2 to 12.5 years. These company-reported figures are also suggestive with respect to the job tenure reported by the study population. For

Table 6-5
Median Age and Job Tenure of the Work Forces of Eight
Participating Employers[a]

Company	Age		Tenure in Years	
	All Employees	Study Population	All Employees	Study Population
A	38.5	50	11.0	9.0
B	39.0	45	12.5	10.0
D	37.1	41	9.2	12.0
I	35.0	41	8.8	5.3
E	38.4	43	7.2	6.7
J	32.0	47	8.1	5.9
H	34.6	39	9.9	8.7
L	39.9	41	9.3	8.1

[a]These figures must be interpreted as suggestive only; the small size of some cells precludes statistical testing.

only one of the eight employers did the job tenure of EHP referrals exceed that of the work force from which they were referred; for the other seven companies, the tenure of EHP workers was shorter than for all employees, even though the latter were, on the average, somewhat younger than EHP referrals.

In summary, even though these findings show no pattern of frequent job turnover among EHP referrals, neither do they suggest a population of alcoholic workers settling inflexibly into their jobs while nonproblem-drinking peers move on to better opportunities elsewhere. Rather, the job tenure of study workers was actually shorter than would be expected on the basis of the longevity experience of workers of similar age and occupation in the same labor force.

Job and Life Satisfaction

The purpose of this section is to determine whether alcoholic workers report greater job dissatisfaction than nonalcoholics in similar work environments. Although a number of investigators have hypothesized a link between job dissatisfaction and drug and alcohol abuse, the evidence is largely conjectural.[3] Consequently, study and comparison workers were asked a range of questions designed to measure their attitudes toward their jobs with respect to overall satisfaction as well as satisfaction with selected aspects of their work and task environments. Additionally, because a number of earlier studies found some evidence of thwarted occupational and life goal attainment among alcoholics, study and comparison workers' responses to questions pertinent to goal attainment are also compared.

Job Satisfaction

Responses to two questions were used to construct a three-point index of overall job satisfaction for purposes of comparing EHP and comparison workers: (1) How much of the time are you satisfied with your job? (2) If you were completely free to go into any type of job you wanted, what would be your choice?[4] As shown in table 6-6, the percentage of respondents falling within each category was remarkably similar for both groups.

When these job satisfaction scores were examined in terms of age, occupation, and race, the findings were consistent with previous studies of job satisfaction. With respect to age, the consistently greater job dissatisfaction among younger workers and greater satisfaction among older workers found by other investigators (Gurin et al. 1960; U.S. Department of Labor 1974) was replicated in the present study. Dissatisfaction decreased and satisfaction increased with age for both the study and comparison groups. Indeed, workers aged twenty to thirty-nine accounted for 65 percent of the job dissatisfaction among EHP

Table 6–6
Job Satisfaction Index

Study Population, %	Comparison Group, %	Job Satisfaction Scores		Responses
39	37	(1) Satisfied	=	Satisfied most or a good deal of the time, and if free to do so, would choose the same type of job again
34	39	(2) Ambivalent	=	Satisfied most or a good deal of the time, but would not choose the same type of job again
27	24	(3) Dissatisfied	=	Satisfied half the time or less, and would not choose the same type of job again

referrals and 60 percent of the job dissatisfaction among the comparison group. By contrast, older workers (aged fifty to sixty-four accounted for only 10 percent of the dissatisfaction among EHP referrals and 8 percent of the dissatisfaction among comparison workers.

Researchers have found that the social-status ranking of an occupation predicts much of the variance in the distribution of job satisfaction scores. Professionals and managers show the greatest amount of job satisfaction, whereas low-status white-collar workers and unskilled blue-collar workers show the least (Robinson 1969). Consistent with the above expectations, in both the study population and the comparison group, professionals and managers were more often satisfied than the group as a whole, and in each age group, laborers and low-status white-collar workers were less often satisfied and more often dissatisfied than other workers. Although a greater percentage of comparison than study operatives and craftsmen fell into the ambivalent category, the percentage of craftsmen and operatives who were dissatisfied was similar in both groups.

The distribution of job satisfaction scores by race was similar in both groups, and there were no signigicant differences between blacks' and whites' responses to questions on job satisfaction when age and occupation were held constant. This finding is consistent with those investigators who have argued that the greater job dissatisfaction among blacks than whites found in several studies is a reflection of the lower-status jobs they hold (O'Toole et al. 1973).

Given that only about one-fourth of the respondents in both groups expressed overall job dissatisfaction, it may be that the respondent's statement that he would choose another job if he were free to do so is a poor proxy for job dissatisfaction for these Baltimore workers. That this might be the case is suggested by the fact that when asked whether they would leave their present job if they could make more money elsewhere, 45 percent of the study population and 48 percent of the comparison group said they would not change jobs, even for more money. Moreover, 30 percent of both study and comparison workers who said that they would not choose the same type of job if they were completely free to go into any type of work they wanted also indicated that they would not leave their present jobs, even for more money. Clearly, these workers did not perceive themselves to be free to change jobs, with the great majority mentioning security or seniority as the reason for not wanting to leave their employer.

A better understanding of the feelings of these workers toward their jobs comes from responses to a series to questions asked of the study population about features of the work situation that have been found to be associated with job dissatisfaction by other investigators (Voom 1964; Sheppard and Herrick 1972). Table 6–7 shows that the percentage of workers who were rarely or never bothered by six features of the work enviornment ranged from 57 to 73 percent. (On the one such question asked of the comparison group—freedom to do your work as you see fit—the percentage distribution of responses was identical to that of the study population.) Even though 71 percent had little variety in their work, only 34 percent found their jobs to be boring at least some of the time. Of those who perceived little chance to get ahead, even though opportunities to learn were good or great (40 percent of respondents), fewer than half were concerned about the lack of advancement potential. When these responses were examined in terms of demographic variables, the results were consistent with those reported earlier; namely, the greatest dissatisfaction was found among the youngest respondents and clerical workers.

Table 6–7
Perceptions of the Study Population Regarding Features of the
Work Environment

	Great or Above Average	Moderate, Little, or None	Respondents Who Are Bothered At Least Some of the Time
	%	%	%
Opportunities to learn	69	31	34
Opportunities to advance	34	66	38
Management's emphasis on quality of output (versus quantity)	52	48	43
Freedom to do work as one sees fit	38	62	27
Variety (or lack of routine)	29	71	34
Amount of boredom experienced on the job	34	66	–

Although a number of recent studies have reported higher levels of job dissatisfaction among the populations they studied (Sheppard and Herrick 1972), it is important to underline that the findings reported here are not at odds with those of other investigators. Overall, the responses of both populations would seem to indicate a fatalistic posture toward what they can realistically expect, rather than a positive feeling that the jobs they hold are among the best to be had. As Robinson (1969) notes,

To many of them [blue-collar workers], just having a job (which provides, besides more money, a certain feeling of membership in society as well as constructive use of time that otherwise would be wasted) makes them highly satisfied. This hardly means that they are ecstatically attached to their jobs; rather their general mood has been well-described as one of "fatalistic" contentment.

That this may well be so for these Baltimore workers was shown in their responses to the question, Would you want your son or daughter to pursue this [your] line or work? Sixty-eight percent of the study population and 73 percent of the comparison group responded in the negative. Moreover, even though more likely to find certain aspects of their jobs dissatisfying, clerical workers in both groups were much more willing to see their children pursue the same type of work they did, and the seemingly contented blue-collar workers wanted better for their children.

The most important aspect of these findings, however, is the similarity between the treatment population of identified alcoholics and nonalcoholics in the same work force, that is, the majority in both groups were not dissatisfied with their jobs and expected little intrinsic satisfaction from them. Despite the consistency in responses on job satisfaction between the two groups, there proved to be a clear difference between alcoholic and nonalcoholic workers in their assessments of their life achievements, as will be discussed below.

Expectations versus Achievement

Previous studies on the relationship between alcoholism and occupational goal attainment have found that alcoholics often had job preferences at variance with the jobs that they actually held (Strayer 1957; Hochwald 1951; Hardy and Cull 1971). To determine whether a similar picture of thwarted occupational goal attainment would be found when alcoholics were compared with non-alcoholics in similar occupations, the study population and comparison group were asked how well their present job measured up to the kind they wanted when they had first taken it. Consistent with their responses to other questions on job satisfaction, 74 percent of the study population and 71 percent of the comparison group said it was like the job they wanted.

However, the first clear attitudinal differences emerged when two questions on overall life goal achievement were put to the two groups: (1) Where are you now compared with what you hoped for when you finished school? (2) Where are you now in relation to the things you wanted out of life compared with ten years ago? Forty-six percent of the alcoholic workers compared with 21 percent of the comparison group, or more than twice as many EHP workers, had experienced frustration in terms of one or both achievement areas.[5] When respondents' perceptions of where they were at the time of interview compared with their hopes when they finished school were examined in terms of age, occupation, and race, differences in the subcategories ranged from 5 to 30 percent fewer study than comparison workers ahead, and from 7 to 23 percent more behind. Similarly, with respect to respondents' perceptions of where they were in relation to ten years ago, 6 to 25 percent more EHP than comparison workers saw themselves as behind, and 15 to 35 percent fewer saw themselves as being ahead.

These findings do suggest a relationship between thwarted ambition and alcohol misuse, but the contribution of work-related goals to overall life frustrations reported by EHP alcoholics remains obscure. Indeed, fewer than half of EHP study workers who said that they had not reached the goals they had had when they finished school reported dissatisfaction with their jobs. But why should alcoholic and nonalcoholic workers differ so greatly in overall goal attainment when the groups are so similar in their reports of job satisfaction? While this question cannot be answered on the basis of the data at hand, it may be hypothesized that although the majority of both groups of workers were occupying positions toward the lower end of the occupational status scale, comparison workers became more resigned to it by lowering their aspirations and finding compensatory satisfactions in other life pursuits. Or perhaps comparison workers had lower expectations from the beginning, never expecting great satisfaction from their life or work roles, and thus were less likely to experience frustrated goals. Conversely, alcoholics may have set higher life goals for themselves, and while not necessarily hating the lower-status jobs they occupied, were unable to compensate by finding satisfaction in other life areas.

Given the long history of heavy drinking reported by the study population, it might be argued that the abuse of alcohol itself was responsible for the failure of many study workers to achieve their goals. If this were the case, however, then the percentage of EHP workers who perceived themselves as being behind where they were ten years ago would probably have been higher. Only 18 percent of EHP workers said they were behind relative to ten years ago, and 59 percent said they were ahead. It would seem more plausible, therefore, that study workers had aspired to upward social mobility when younger, but were thwarted by larger societal barriers that act to perpetuate preexisting class and occupational positions. In fact, the tendency of many individuals in the lower and working classes to see themselves as fixed in life situations of relative disadvantage has been implicated as a major factor accounting for the poorer mental health found among lower-status than higher-status persons (Kornhauser 1965).

Even though the above argument is consistent with the hypothesis of McClelland et al. (1972) that heavy drinkers are persons having strong power needs, it is, of course, highly speculative. Respondents were not asked what their specific goals were, and it is equally possible that what EHP study workers hoped for when they left school was not upward social mobility at all, but success in more practical areas, such as greater material wealth or better inter-personal relationships. However, the data presented in this section definitely do not indicate a relationship between job dissatisfaction and alcoholism among industrial workers. What they do suggest is that investigations into factors promoting alcohol abuse in employed populations should examine job satisfaction within the context of larger life goals and achievements.

7

Job Retention and Clinic Attendance of the Study Population

Evaluations of the effectiveness of treating workers in industrial alcoholism programs have employed a number of criteria, including job maintenance, drinking behavior, and supervisors' evaluations as well as changes in specific aspects of work performance (e.g., absenteeism, accidents, and promotions) as measures of possible improvement due to treatment. As discussed in chapter 1, extensive follow-up of patients treated at EHP could not be completed, and data on specific changes in drinking and employment performance are not available to us. However, since the major goal of treatment was to retain problem drinkers on the job, data on the employment and treatment continuation status of EHP workers eight to thirty months after referral are presented in the first part of this chapter that, while lacking in detail, suggest favorable results from treatment similar to those achieved by other industrial alcoholism programs.

Using this data on job retention and treatment continuation status as indicators of treatment outcome, the balance of this chapter is devoted to an exploratory analysis of the correlates of EHP workers' treatment experiences. While in themselves inadequate for making inferences about other industrial alcoholism treatment populations, these data suggest hypotheses that might be examined in future research. Given the exploratory nature of this analysis, we make no attempts to assess the significance of the differences we found.

Job Retention and Treatment Continuation
Status at Follow-up

Table 7-1, which gives the employment status of the study population as of February 15, 1976, shows that 81.4 percent were still working for the employers who referred them. Comparing the experience of EHP patients with that of private utility workers referred for clinic treatment under a company alcoholism program (Franco 1960), table 7-2 shows that 79 percent of EHP patients (excluding those referred less than one year ago) versus 60 percent of Consolidated Edison referrals were still on the job at the time of review. Of course, Franco's data, which cover a period of two to five years following referral, are not strictly comparable since they also take into account employment changes occurring after the second year. However, Franco noted that 65 percent of all patients who lost their jobs did so within the first year following referral, suggesting that subsequent years will produce additional job losses, but not a

Table 7-1
Employment Status of Study Population on February 15, 1976

Employment Status	Number of Months since Referral				All Patients
	24-30	18-23	12-17	8-11	
Number retained by referring employer					
Employed at same job	34	36	50	27	147
Reinstated	–	4	9	2	15 83.3% employed
Number terminated by referring employer					
Not rehired; another job	–	–	2	–	2
Terminated after beginning treatment; another job	2	1	2	–	5
Not rehired; unemployed	1	1	5	1	8
Terminated after beginning treatment; unemployed	7	8	7	–	22
Percentage retained	77.3%	80.0%	78.6%	96.7%	81.4%
Percentage retained excluding self-referrals	76.3%	76.7%	77.3%	85.1%	79.9%
Other					
Quit job; unemployed	1	–	2	1	4
Decreased; retired	1	2	–	–	3

Table 7-2

Comparison of Treatment and Job Retention Experiences of Two Treatment Populations

Status of Patient	Franco[a] (1952–1957) 1–5 Years		EHP (1973–1975) 1–2 1/2 Years	
	n	%	n	%
Patients referred to clinic[b]	190	–	163	–
Patients completing one year of treatment	128	67.0	67	41
Dropouts from treatment	62	33.0	96	59
Patients continuing treatment who maintained jobs	87	68.0	61	91
Dropouts who maintained jobs	27	43.5	68	71
All patients who kept jobs	114[c]	60.0	129	79

[a]Franco (1960). These cases were reviewed in March 1957; thus, each patient had been referred at least two years prior to review.

[b]Excludes patients who were referred outside clinic, and those who retired or quit their jobs.

[c]Sixty-five percent of those who lost their jobs did so within the first year of follow-up. After the fourth year, relapses with failure and loss of jobs are rare.

dramatic number. Table 7-1, which breaks down the EHP study population into six-month periods since referral, shows only a substantial difference in job retention for the group referred less than a year before follow-up. Thus, there was little difference in employment status between workers referred twelve months and those referred thirty months before follow-up, suggesting that, over the long run, EHP referrals will do as well if not better in job retention than Franco's private utility workers.

This high percentage of job retention by EHP referrals is similar to that reported in more recent studies of job status after referral to treatment in industrial alcoholism programs. Kamner and Dupong (1969) reported that 80 percent of 300 patients who were referred to their New York Telephone Company's medical department for alcoholism treatment kept their jobs, but this figure also includes workers who were terminated for reasons other than alcoholism, or who left voluntarily. By contrast, the retention percentages reported for EHP workers include all those discharged for any reason, and exclude voluntary terminations on the assumption that workers may have quit in preference to undergoing treatment or to being fired.

Additionally, Clyne (1965) reviewed 107 workers referred over a three-year period, of whom 85 percent retained their jobs, but this figure combines recent as well as earlier referrals. Finally, Smart (1974) reported that 81 percent of workers referred for clinic treatment under threat of job loss were still working for the same employer one year after referral. Smart's figures, as EHP's, include only those who stayed in treatment on the job compared with those who were dismissed.

Another aspect of EHP treatment for which data are available is whether or not patients stayed in treatment or dropped out before one year. Table 7-3 shows that of all workers in the study population who were referred to treatment twelve to thirty months before review on February 15, 1976, 38.3 percent were either considered to have successfully completed treatment by EHP counselors or were still actively attending the clinic. The table shows that the percentage of dropouts declined from a high of 70 percent during the period before clinic relocation (or the first two six-month periods shown on the table) and remained steady at approximately 50 percent in the period following relocation. This underscores the influence that moving the clinic in October 1974 had in making it more accessible to EHP patients (see the discussion on clinic relocation in chapter 2, p. 17). Thus, it would seem reasonable to consider as standard the 50 percent dropout figure characterizing the postrelocation period.

While this dropout rate is higher than that reported for Consolidated Edison workers (33 percent, as shown in table 7-2), we do not know whether the rate found by Franco was exceptionally low or EHP's exceptionally high, compared with other alcoholism programs.[1] Unfortunately, none of the other more than twenty studies we reviewed indicated how many workers dropped out of treatment. It can be argued, however, that the patients studied by Franco were

Table 7-3
Treatment Status of Study Population on February 15, 1976

| Treatment Status | Number of Months since Referral | | | | |
	24-30	18-23	12-17	8-11	Total
Number who successfully completed treatment	4	2	7	–	13
Number who were actively attending clinic	9	14	31	16	70
Number who had dropped out of treatment	31	35	36	15	117
Number who had been referred elsewhere	2	1	3	0	6
Percentage of patients active in or completing treatment[a]	29.5%	31.4%	51.4%	51.6%	41.5%
		38.3%			

[a]Calculation excludes patients referred to other clinics, AA, or hospitals.

referred under circumstances highly conducive to clinic attendance. All patients referred for clinic treatment under the Consolidated Edison program were put on probation while in treatment and were under clear threat of job loss if they did not show substantial improvement in job performance. Referral was to a single clinic at a university hospital that was launched with company funds, and the company's medical department continuously monitored patients throughout treatment.

Nevertheless, EHP's attendance record is considerably better than that achieved by other outpatient alcoholism clinics servicing primarily employed, socially stable patient populations. In reporting treatment results obtained in two outpatient clinics and one hospital rehabilitation ward in which patients received outpatient follow-up after discharge, Kissin et al. (1968) were only able to locate 50 percent of the cases one year after registration. However, of those they were able to follow up, only 35 percent had made as many as eleven visits. Similarly, in a survey of eight outpatient clinics, Gerard and Saenger (1966) found that only about one in four patients maintained contract with the clinic for six months or longer subsequent to intake. Finally, preliminary findings of the Industrial Alcoholism Center (IAC) Evaluation Program (Stanford Research Institute 1974) reveal dropout rates ranging from 60 to 90 percent, with an overall dropout rate of 75 percent for the five IAC clinics in the nine months since they began to accept patients under the evaluation program. While EHP differs from the above clinics in servicing a defined population of problem-drinking workers, the experiences of these clinics illustrate the dropout problem inherent in outpatient treatment.

One additional finding regarding clinic attendance by EHP workers should be noted here, namely, the relationship between staying in treatment and remaining on the job. Table 7-4 shows that those EHP patients who stayed in treatment for one year or longer were 20 percent more likely to keep their jobs than those who dropped out. Moreover, 95.5 percent of those who continued treatment were still in the labor force at the time of review, versus 75 percent of the dropouts. These results agree with Franco's findings that 68 percent of Consolidated Edison patients who continued treatment retained their jobs, whereas only 43.5 percent of the dropouts were able to keep theirs.

Exploratory Analysis of Correlates of Treatment Outcomes

Because the number of EHP workers not retained by referring employers was so small, it was difficult to discern characteristics which might distinguish between treatment "successes" and "failures" on the criterion of job retention. Indeed, as will be seen in the discussion below, even for the few workers who were actually terminated, differences in policy toward discipline and discharge among referring companies might have been as much a determinant of retention as the

Table 7–4
Relationship between Remaining in Treatment and Employment Status,
February 15, 1976

	Employment Status		
Treatment Status of Patients Referred on or Before February 15, 1975	Number Retained by Employer	Number Terminated by Employer	Percentage Retained by Employer
Active or completed treatment	61	6[a]	91%
Dropped out[b]	68	28[c]	71%
Referred elsewhere	4	2	–

[a]Includes three now employed elsewhere.

[b]Excludes six who quit, retired, or died.

[c]Includes four now employed elsewhere.

characteristics of the workers themselves. Consequently, remaining in treatment will also be considered as a proxy for treatment success. While we recognize that evaluation of the actual degree of success achieved by EHP treatment cannot be made, prognostic evaluations of treatment outcomes show a high correlation between length of contact and ultimate treatment success (Gerard and Saenger 1966).

In this exploratory analysis of correlates of treatment outcome we look at a number of the variables found to be associated with treatment outcomes by other investigators (Trice et al. 1969; Gerard and Saenger 1966; Kissin et al 1968), comparing EHP workers who were retained by their employers with those who were discharged, and workers who continued in treatment with those who dropped out. We then examine the possible relationship between treatment outcomes and type of employer (civil service versus private industry) and between treatment outcomes and attitudes toward referral and treatment.

Characteristics of Workers and Treatment Outcomes

Table 7-5 shows the differences between retained and discharged workers with respect to occupation and job tenure. While the numbers are small, the figures on job retention by occupation are interesting, especially within the blue-collar occupations where it would appear that skilled and semiskilled blue-collar workers were at greater risk of being terminated than unskilled service workers and laborers. One explanation might be that the poor performance of higher-level blue-collar workers is more disruptive than that of laborers. But another possibility is suggested by Warkov et al. (1965), who found that the performance of skilled problem-drinking workers was judged more harshly than that of less skilled problem-drinking workers. They attributed this phenomenon to differentials in tolerance of deviance according to status, with supervisors more frequently severe in passing judgment on employees approaching them in rank.

Table 7-5 also shows that a higher percentage of discharged than retained workers fell below the median job tenure (ten years) of the study population. It is not surprising that employers would be less likely to discharge workers with long service to the firm. However, the likelihood of long-tenured workers being retained was not associated with skill level. Of the fourteen long-tenured workers discharged, two were professionals, one was a clerical worker, and eleven were craftsmen or operatives.

When workers staying in treatment were compared with those who dropped out, there were no apparent differences between groups with respect to race, education, state of birth, job tenure, job satisfaction, age when heavy drinking began, previous contact with AA, achievement/aspiration, or drinking pattern (periodic versus chronic). As expected, Protestant religion was a differentiating variable, but unlike in Kissin et al. (1968), for whites rather than blacks. While about 15 percent of blacks among both dropouts and continuing patients were Protestants, 20 percent more whites who continued were Protestants than those who dropped out. For both races no religion was found primarily among dropouts, with 11 percent more black and 16 percent more white dropouts than continuing patients reporting no religion.

As expected, being married and living with one's spouse was related to staying in treatment. However, single patients occurred in equal proportion in both groups of patients, the difference being in the greater proportion of widowed,

Table 7-5
Occupation and Job Tenure of Discharged Workers

	Discharged		Retained	
Occupation	*n*	*%*	*n*	*%*
Professionals/managers	(2)	13	(13)	87
Clerical/sales	(4)	15	(22)	85
Craftsmen	(10)	29	(25)	71
Operatives	(16)	30	(38)	70
Service workers	(1)	5	(18)	95
Laborers	(4)	8	(47)	92
Total	(37)		(163)	
Tenure				
Less than 10	(23)	62	(70)	43
Greater than or equal to 10	(14)	38	(93)	57
Total	(37)	100	(163)	100

separated, and divorced patients among dropouts. With respect to years of heavy drinking, the least favorable category for staying in treatment was less than five years. This finding is supported by Trice et al. (1969), who found a longer period of alcoholism to be associated with treatment success. Parallel to this finding, since years of heavy drinking are closely related to age, workers in the youngest age group were more likely to drop out of treatment than older workers.

Treatment other than AA was twice as common among continuing patients than among dropouts, while, as suggested above, equal percentages of both groups of patients had had contact with AA prior to referral to EHP. This latter finding is not surprising, considering that only about 10 percent of EHP patients reporting previous contact with AA had sustained it for more than a year.

Three variables we examined yielded surprising findings. While white-collar and skilled occupations have been shown to be related to favorable treatment outcomes by other investigators, only among EHP professional and managerial workers did this association hold, with laborers and service workers more unlikely and clerical workers, craftsmen, and operatives more likely to drop out. It may well be that continuing treatment associated with improved job performance for these lower-status blue-collar workers contributed to their higher rates of job retention. But the numbers are small, and in the absence of follow-up data on job performance, this is merely a guess.

Finally, both exposure to problem drinking at home and more than two prior arrests were associated with workers who continued treatment when just the opposite would have been predicted on the basis of past investigations. More continuing patients than dropouts had grown up in a home in which a family member had a drinking problem, and more continuing patients had reported three or more arrests. However, the differences are small, and the extent to which prior arrests were for juvenile offense occurring many years earlier is not known.

In summary, practicing a religion, being married as opposed to being widowed, divorced, or separated, five to nineteen years of heavy drinking, ages thirty-five to fifty-four, prior treatment for alcoholism, and being a professional, service worker, or laborer were more often characteristic of workers who continued treatment than those who dropped out. However, a number of factors found to be associated with favorable treatment outcomes by other investigators either proved not to differentiate EHP workers who stayed in treatment, or did so, but in the opposite way predicted. While in some cases the reason might be the small numbers involved, for example, only a small percentage of the overall population were periodic drinkers, the main explanation is probably the difference in populations. In populations presenting a wider mix of socioeconomic status, multifactorial analyses will tend to find much of the variance explained by factors that are concomitants of higher-social status which—on the basis of previous studies and as shown in the limited experience of EHP in treating professional and managerial workers—would appear to be in itself among the most powerful predictors of alcoholism treatment success. However, when the population is predominantly of one social-class level, that is, working or lower-middle class, factors such as state hospitalizations and prior arrests, which are characteristic of the group as a whole, may not produce any marked differences among subgroups within the population.

Characteristics of Employers

It is a widely held view that civil service employees are protected from job separation to a greater extent than workers in private industry where competition and "the profit motive" impinge more directly upon the work force. This did appear to be the case for EHP referrals; civil service employers referred almost one-third of the study population but accounted for only one-fifth of the terminations.

However, this finding does not necessarily mean that substantially more EHP workers would be without jobs had they all worked for private companies. For example, companies C and D, who together referred almost one-half of the study population fired 21 percent and retained 79 percent of the workers they referred. This is very similar to the overall job retention rate of 81.4 percent. Another factor, that is, referrals by nonparticipating companies, explains much of the difference in the greater proportion of terminations by private companies. Throughout clinic operation, the EHP project staff continued to encourage other employers to become members and, as a result, a number of companies agreed to refer workers to EHP on a "trial basis." The fact that these companies were not bound by the informal promise to retain workers undergoing treatment is revealed by the following figures: of the fifteen workers referred by nonmember companies, eight (53 percent) were ultimately discharged from their jobs. Indeed, if the patients referred by these companies are not taken into account, the percentage of overall job retention rises from 81.4 to 84.2 percent. Thus, although civil service participating employers did fire a smaller percentage of referred workers than their private industry counterparts, the overall percentage of workers retained is not biased substantially upward as a result.

Voluntary versus Coerced Referral and Attitudes
toward Treatment

As discussed in chapter 4, favorable treatment results have been reported whether the patient is referred under threat of job loss (i.e., "coerced") or whether he comes to treatment as a voluntary. However, in the one study which has compared voluntary and mandatory referrals in a company alcoholism treatment program, more of the highly motivated self-referrals showed improvement due to treatment than those referred under constructive confrontation (Smart 1974). Thus, it was of interest to compare the experiences of self-referred and coerced EHP workers with respect to job retention and clinic attendance.

Table 7-1 shows that when self-referrals are excluded, the overall percentage of job retention is only 1.5 percent lower, or 79.9 percent as against 81.4 percent. Interestingly, the EHP patients who came to the clinic on their own had a slightly higher dropout rate than the population as a whole in the period prior to clinic relocation (75 percent for self-referrals compared with 70 percent overall). After clinic relocation, self-referred patients had approximately the same dropout rate (50 percent) as all other patients. While these findings would appear to indicate little difference between self-referrals and coerced referrals either in job retention or in clinic attendance, it should be remembered that some self-referrals also perceived themselves as being at risk of job loss.

Another aspect of motivation for treatment is patients' attitudes toward the circumstances surrounding their referral as well as their recognition of the seriousness of their drinking problem. To assess how serious a problem the workers felt their drinking to be, four questions comprising the NIAAA's self-perception index (Stanford Research Institute 1974) were put to the study population. The component questions of the index and the scores attached to each are shown in table 7-6. To determine whether differential attitudes and motivations of patients toward their drinking and toward therapeutic intervention at intake are associated with differential treatment outcomes, table 7-7 compares the self-perception index scores and the overall dispositions toward referral and treatment (see chapter 5, p. 64) of EHP patients who continued in treatment with those of patients who dropped out.

Table 7-7 shows that 10 percent more of the patients who continued treatment perceived themselves to have a serious or moderately serious drinking problem (a score of 6 or higher) upon intake than did clinic dropouts. Also, the table shows patients' attitudes toward the referral, with the negative category including patients who felt that the referral was inappropriate or who saw no need for treatment. Again, patients with negative attitudes toward referral or treatment were more likely to drop out of treatment.

It would appear, then, that both attitudes toward treatment and self-perceptions of drinking at intake are related to continuation of treatment. However, workers with low scores on self-perceived drinking problems were only a quarter of the population, and workers adverse to referral comprised only 23 percent of all workers referred under constructive confrontation. Thus, while EHP patients' attitudes at the time of intake were related to treatment outcome, the confrontation strategy did not prove to be a substantial barrier to the workers' acceptance of treatment.

Table 7-6
Self-Perception Index[a]

Component Questions	Score
How would you, yourself, describe your drinking at the present time?	
I don't drink.	= 0
I am a social drinker.	= 1
Sometimes I drink more than I should.	= 2
I have a steady drinking problem.	= 3
At the moment, how serious a problem do you feel your drinking is?	
It is no problem at all.	= 0
It is a slight problem.	= 1
It is a moderate problem.	= 2
It is a serious problem.	= 3
During the past month, would you say that your drinking problem:	
Has improved.	= 0
Stayed the same.	= 1
Gotten worse.	= 2
What do you think you will be able to do in the next few months about your drinking problem?	
Drink more.	= 0
Stay the same.	= 1
Cut down.	= 2
Stop altogether.	= 3

[a]The maximum score is 11 and the minimum score is 0. (From Stanford Research Institute 1974.)

Table 7-7
Self-Perception, Attitude toward Referral, and Treatment Outcome

	Continued Treatment			Dropped Out	
	n	*%*	*n*	*%*	
Self-perception Scores					
10–11	(19)	23		(16)	13
8–9	(22)	27	80	(38)	31 70
6–7	(25)	30		(32)	26
4–5	(8)	10		(22)	18
2–3	(8)	10	20	(12)	10 30
0–1	(0)	0		(3)	2
	(82)	100		(123)	100
Attitude toward Referral and Need for Treatment[a]					
Positive	(58)	81		(80)	74
Negative	(14)	19		(28)	26
	(72)	100		(108)	100

[a]Excludes self-referrals

Summary and Recommendations

The preceding chapters outlined the growth and development of the Employee Health Program (EHP) as a social action program and presented a substantial body of new evidence on the demographic, work-role, and drinking characteristics of a treatment population of problem-drinking workers. This chapter attempts an overview of the major findings reported in earlier chapters. The first section summarizes demonstration findings and the second section, research findings; in the final section a number of conclusions are drawn and policy suggestions are offered on the basis of EHP experience.

Demonstration Findings

With takeover of the EHP clinic on October 31, 1975, by the AFL-CIO's Community Service Department, the project had fulfilled its two most basic demonstration goals: to determine the feasibility of establishing a single-situs alcoholism treatment facility to treat workers of a number of employers and unions, and to determine whether such a multiparty facility could achieve local sponsorship after the expiration of federal funding. The project's experiences in meeting these goals not only suggest the steps involved in establishing a workable program shared by multiple employers and unions, but also clarify a number of issues specific to the operation of multiparty industrial alcoholism programs as well as the more general issues surrounding intervention in workers' alcohol misuse through their employment settings. Following a summary of the steps involved in establishing the clinic as a viable treatment resource, this section outlines the major findings to emerge from the demonstration experience.

Establishing a New Treatment Facility

While community acceptance is always a problem for new alcoholism treatment programs, partly because of the social infrastructure of the preexisting treatment community and partly because of the natural competition for patients, in retrospect, several steps seemed to facilitate the ability of EHP to gain acceptance as a legitimate treatment resource. The first was to become connected with the loosely organized but immensely important social network of Alcoholics Anonymous. Second, the program made clear that its intention was to generate new referrals from a specific catchment population and not to "raid" the patient populations served by existing programs. Third, it was necessary to build alliances with several powerful alcoholism interest groups during the early phases of the project. The issue of community acceptance of the program cannot be understated, since without it, the project might have experienced greater difficulty in securing the cooperation of participating employers and unions, many of whom had had ties with the local alcoholism treatment community antedating their involvement in EHP.

Another factor which appeared to foster the clinic's acceptability to employers and unions was its image of providing high-quality medical care to referred workers. The provision of medical diagnosis and treatment as an integral part of each patient's therapeutic regimen not only furthered its acceptance by the referring parties but also proved to be a key factor in securing both accreditation as well as third-party reimbursement for clinic services. In practice, however, counseling, both individual and group, encompassed a much greater proportion of the patient's treatment experience than did the provision of medical services. Because the physician input required was so small relative to that provided by counselors, the responsibility for administration originally entrusted to a physician was transferred to the counseling staff in the second year of clinic operation. Not only did this arrangement prove to be less costly, but it also eliminated the problem that the clinic's executive committee had had in making the physician-director conform to their policies and procedures.

A factor also proving to be critical to the program's growth and development was the location of the clinic. Toward the end of the first year of clinic operation it became clear that the original clinic location was ill-suited to the needs of the developing patient population, and as such served to discourage both referrals and return visits. Consequently, the clinic was moved to a new location closer to the patients' places of residence and employment. The dramatic improvement in revisit rates following the move underscored the importance of accessibility of outpatient treatment for employed patients.

The final step for ensuring the project's viability was securing an independent source of funding for clinic services. While the development of third-party coverage was a multifaceted process, two factors appeared to have been key to the project's success in fulfilling this major demonstration goal. The first was the presence of a sympathetic insurance carrier—Maryland Blue Cross—that had had prior interest and experience in extending benefits for alcoholism treatment in the form of inpatient coverage. The second, and more important, was that EHP presented a group of potential subscribers (participating unions) ready and willing to purchase the coverage. In addition to providing a source of independent funding necessary to support the clinic after termination of demonstration funds, EHP's pioneering role in developing third-party coverage for outpatient alcoholism treatment services represents a step toward overcoming the barrier that direct employer or union funding has posed to the development of industrial alcoholism programs.

Issues in the Identification and Referral Process

One of the most consistent findings in the literature on company alcoholism treatment programs is the tendency of the identification and referral mechanism to select out lower-status workers disproportionate to their numbers in the work force as a whole. EHP's experience was no exception—the clinic population was predominantly blue collar, with an overrepresentation of unskilled workers. While the implications of the working class clinic clientele will be addressed in the recommendations below, it is important to underline here that the emergence of union rather than employer sponsorship of the clinic is largely explicable in light of the concentration of union-member patients.

Another persistent theme in the literature is the failure of company referral systems to identify workers early in the problem-drinking cycle. Here, too, the project's experience was not different, with referred workers in relatively advanced stages of problem drinking. Because the study population were among the first workers to be referred under the companies' involvement in the program, it is not surprising that their problems were relatively severe. However, some findings from the supervisors' interviews shed additional light on this issue. The majority of EHP supervisors who were interviewed identified workers primarily on the basis of visible signs of problem drinking, even though the technique of constructive confrontation adopted, in principle, by participating employers was that problem drinking be identified on the basis of signs of impaired job performance. Moreover, a common sentiment among the supervisors was their frustration with company policy against directly confronting the worker with his drinking problem. This finding would tend to suggest that supervisors do not anticipate referring workers unless they are convinced beforehand that the problem is alcoholism.

Another aspect of the identification and referral mechanism concerns different organizational models for moving patients into treatment. While EHP participating firms evolved a variety of different systems—from medical-department-dominant to management-union-cooperative—no one system could be identified as superior in its ability to produce referrals. More important than the structure or form of the referral system was the presence of at least one person in the company specifically assigned to deal with alcoholism problems. Indeed, it was the project's experience that in companies having no staff member charged with facilitating clinic-company interaction, referral was virtually impossible, regardless of the announced commitment of cooperation with the project from the highest levels within the organization.

Finally, the importance of policy guidelines for institutionalizing the referral mechanism has been a long accepted tenet among company alcoholism program developers. The results of interviews with EHP supervisors confirmed the desirability of a formal company policy. The supervisors whose company did have specified policies and procedures reported following a relatively straightforward and consistent method of referral once the problem drinker had come to their attention.

Issues of Union-Management Involvement

Among the major demonstration goals set by the project was to develop co-operation between labor and management regarding the referral of workers to treatment for alcohol problems. Unlike most company alcoholism programs in which the role of the union is seen as secondary to that of management, in formulating EHP, unions were envisioned as being coequal to management and, as such, were encouraged to participate fully in identifying the referring workers to treatment. But even though unions were active supporters of the EHP concept and became the long-range sponsors of the program, for the most part, union cooperation during the demonstration phase took the form of reaction to management initiative rather than actively participating in the identification and referral process. While many referrals were made by union officials, the great majority of these took place after other attempts at assistance had failed, that is, either to stave off or to reverse a termination decision. This EHP experience tends to suggest that labor is unlikely to play a strong role in the goal of early identification. Union officials' fears that referring workers to treatment might cost them reelection or would place them at risk of having to testify in an arbitration hearing appeared to be the major reasons for union reluctance to refer.

The major commitment made by participating employers in effecting cooperation with labor in the EHP project was managements' informal promise not to discharge a worker who had agreed to treatment to help correct his alcohol-related poor work performance. As was discussed earlier in this report, participating employers did live up to that commitment. However, some employers also proved to be a factor limiting the number of referrals to the program. In fact, about half of the original twelve participating companies or agencies generated very few referrals throughout the demonstration period, or referred several workers upon first joining, only to reduce substantially or to cease altogether their referral activity over time. Although the tendency to refer the most easily identifiable, that is, most advanced, cases first may have been a contributing factor, it appears that a number of participating employers attached little or no priority to their alcoholism program or involvement in the project. Some employers were not committed to raising "alcoholism consciousness" in their work forces to a level sufficient to produce a large number of referrals. In fact, for a number of employers, the decision to participate was made by high-level management, probably in response to pressures exerted by headquarters for all branch offices and installations to join in the corporation's wider alcoholism policy. Finally, and it could be argued most importantly, the decision of employers to participate in EHP represented a different order of commitment to alcoholism identification and referral from that implied by a single company's decision to initiate and finance a program. Thus, even a management strongly committed to rehabilitation would, in all likelihood, have a greater stake in the success of a program that it controls than one in which it only participates.

The Question of Constituency Support

At the outset of the demonstration, it was anticipated that management enthusiasm for a referral and treatment facility for alcoholic workers would be such that participating employers would eventually provide financial support for the clinic effort. This expectation proved wrong despite the expressions of support from managements upon first joining the program and the thrust of alcoholism literature pointing to the receptiveness of employers to arguments of cost savings which would persuade them to underwrite treatment programs as an investment in retaining skilled workers. However, strong management support for the project of a nature that could provide for its continued support never developed. The twelve managements did not have a mechanism to form a unified group which could make an offer of support. This reflected both the institutional difficulties of managements cooperating in a nonbusiness-related problem as well as the relatively low priority given to alcoholism treatment within each firm. Additionally, managements were not persuaded that treatment would yield cost savings sufficient to justify the investment of organizational resources in alcoholism treatment. Indeed, given the virtual disregard by management of questions of cost-effectiveness in the negotiations regarding clinic takeover, it seems likely that cost considerations were at the very most a secondary motivation for their participation in the project. In addition to the fact that workers referred to the program were occupying relatively low-skill-level positions, all of the participating organizations were engaged in process-type manufacture of goods or services and in which the diminshed contribution of any one worker is difficult to assess.

While a structure for facilitating the cooperation necessary to operate the clinic was absent among employers, participating unions had a natural bond for cooperation as well as a clearly identifiable interest in overseeing the treatment provided to their members. Moreover, the question of cost-effectiveness of treatment does not even arise for unions that can justify expenditures such as those required to operate EHP on the basis of the humanitarian motive of extending the health and welfare concerns of member workers.

Research Findings

In addition to presenting a large body of descriptive findings on the sociodemographic, work history, and drinking characteristics of EHP workers, the study population was compared with nonproblem drinkers in the same work force to determine the extent to which they differed with respect to social and labor force stability. Although the social stability of study workers compared favorably with that of other treatment populations of employed problem drinkers, EHP referrals showed significantly less social and labor force stability than the comparison group of nonproblem drinkers. This finding diverges from much of the emphasis in the occupational alcoholism literature, which often imples that alcoholic employees are even more stable than their "normal" counterparts. Although EHP workers were far from conforming to the image of the skid-row alcoholic, when compared with their peers of nonproblem drinkers, it becomes clear that alcohol misuse does have an impact on several spheres of normal life functioning.

Because of a growing number of studies suggesting a relationship between drinking and drug abuse problems and stresses and dissatisfactions related to work roles, the present study compared responses of EHP workers with those of nonproblem-drinking comparison workers to a wide range of questions on job satisfaction. Despite the predicted association between job dissatisfaction and alcohol misuse, study workers' attitudes toward their jobs were very similar to those reported by comparison workers when age, race, and occupation were taken into account. On the basis of these findings, the hypothesis that job attitudes and satisfactions of problem drinkers differ from those of nonproblem drinkers cannot be accepted. However, there were substantial differences between study and comparison workers on their assessments of overall life goal attainments, with twice as many EHP alcoholic workers reporting frustration in goal attainment. A possible explanation for this latter difference was offered that could be subjected to further scrutiny in subsequent investigations. In summary, it was argued that although the majority of both study and comparison workers were occupying positions toward the lower end of the occupational status scale, comparison workers may have become more resigned to it by lowering their aspirations and finding compensatory satisfactions in other life pursuits. Conversely, alcoholics may have set higher life goals for themselves, and while not necessarily hating the lower-status jobs they occupied, were unable to compensate by finding satisfaction in other life areas.

Data on the employment status of EHP workers collected on February 15, 1976, showed that 81.4 percent of the study population were still working for the employer they had at the time of referral, and 83.3 percent were still active members of the labor force. Previous investigations have found that most recidivism occurs within the first year of referral. Since job retention rates of EHP referrals differed little between workers referred twelve months and those referred thirty months before the time of review, it is reasonable to conclude that over time the percentage of EHP workers retained by their employers will not be substantially lower than those reported above. The rate of job retention experienced by workers who remained in treatment was considerably higher than that of workers who dropped out before one year. The percentages of job retention by study workers compare favorably with those reported in several other studies of treatment outcomes for populations of employed problem drinkers.

Because the number of workers terminated by their referring employers was so small, it was impossible to determine differences between retained and discharged workers on most variables examined. While workers terminated did have a shorter period of job tenure than the study population as a whole, the lowest-tenured workers among those discharged were concentrated in occupational categories of laborer and service, while skilled and clerical workers discharged tended to have tenures exceeding the median for the study population. This finding adds further weight to the argument that cost-benefit considerations, as measured by the company's investment in a highly skilled employee, appear to have little bearing on the orientation of EHP participating employers toward treatment of alcoholic workers.

Using continuance in treatment as a proxy for treatment success and as a predictor for ultimate job retention, workers staying in treatment were compared with dropouts in terms of several variables found to be predictors of treatment success by other investigators. Workers who continued in treatment were more likely to practice a religion, to be married and living with their spouse, to have had a longer period of heavy drinking prior to intake, to be age thirty-five or older, to have had prior treatment for alcoholism, and to be professionals, service workers, or laborers. This latter finding of greater clinic continuance by lower-status EHP workers among the blue-collar occupations runs contrary to findings of other prognostic studies, and a number of variables found to be predictors of success in other studies were more often associated with EHP dropouts (i.e., failures) than EHP treatment continuers. Indeed, the EHP workers who did continue in treatment had characteristics that other investigators have found to be associated with poor treatment outcomes. Additionally, when the percentages of workers retained and terminated were examined in light of characteristics of the employer, it was found that civil service employers were less likely to terminate a worker after identification than were private employers.

When the impact of patients' receptivity to treatment, in general, as well as the influence of the mode of referral (i.e., coerced versus voluntary) on workers' acceptance of treatment were examined, it was found that workers with negative attitudes toward referral or treatment as well as workers who perceived themselves as having little or no problem with alcohol were much more likely to drop out of treatment than were workers favorably disposed to referral and treatment. What is more interesting, however, is that fewer than one-fourth of patients referred via constructive confrontation had negative attitudes toward referral or treatment, suggesting that the confrontation strategy is not a formidable barrier to a worker's acceptance of treatment. Also noteworthy is that self-referrals did only slightly better on job retention (and had just as high a dropout rate from treatment) than workers referred under constructive confrontation.

Conclusions and Recommendations

The very existence of the EHP project was predicated upon the potential labor market problem presented by alcoholism among workers. Putting aside for a moment the economics of treatment and the question of where the burden for financing it properly falls, there is the reality of a significant segment of the working population having serious problems from alcohol misuse. Evidence presented by investigators with access to populations not restricted to who is identified and referred, suggests that the percentage of black workers suffering from alcoholism is higher than that of white workers and the proportion of blue-collar workers so afflicted may exceed that of white-collar employees. If this is the case, it may well be that alcohol abuse among workers, such as those seen at EHP, while providing a psychic means to avoid the realization of not participating in the "American dream" of upward mobility for the individual, could itself be the precipitant for a subsegment of the American labor force to be separated from full work force participation. The importance of the work role to the individual's psychological and physical health cannot be minimized in our society. Much of overall social identity and status devolves from it. As a result, alcoholic blue-collar workers may easily see themselves as double losers—first, occupying the lowest-status positions in the occupational hierarchy and, second, as alcoholics, with no hope for gaining more meaningful work or a responsible place in society. To abandon this population is to allow the eventual loss of their potential output and contribution to the economy and to continue the cyclical process which keeps disadvantaged minorities in powerless and fixed positions. EHP experience has shown that intervention in the problem-drinking cycle does appear to increase the labor market stability of a large majority of workers treated.

Among the major implications of the EHP demonstration experience is that the multiparty approach could be a viable model for organizing treatment services for working alcoholics, provided that long-term funding can be guaranteed. Although the rate of referrals to the clinic was slow initially, once the major hurdles of community resistance, clinic reorganization, and clinic relocation had been surpassed, referrals began to grow and this growth persisted long after direct efforts to stimulate them through the liaison network had been terminated. Moreover, the multiparty model, by concentrating a complete set of referral, counseling, and treatment resources in one facility whose sole purpose is providing care to employed alcoholics, may be better able to deliver the highest quality of care available than a series of many in-house programs not able to offer as wide a range of treatment services and professional expertise.

However, in recommending the multiparty approach as a model that future treatment efforts should adopt, it is important to stress that the constituency support required to sustain such a single-situs treatment concept may be restricted to organized labor. The multiparty treatment concept requires a structure that transcends a physical clinic or facility. While such a structure is inherent in organized labor, there is no management analog to the AFL-CIO's Community Services Department. Given the limited resources that EHP companies were willing to commit to the project, even when such a structure was made available to them, it is unlikely the employers elsewhere would be prepared to invest in effecting the linkages that a multiparty program requires.

Based on the eagerness of the AFL-CIO unions to sponsor the EHP treatment effort in Baltimore as well as the growing active involvement of labor at the national level in encouraging locals and affiliates to take a more aggressive role in alcoholism treatment, it would seem that there already exists an infrastructure for the diffusion of industrial treatment programs that can act independently of criteria of cost-effectiveness. Additionally, EHP has demonstrated that insurance reimbursement of outpatient treatment for employed alcoholics is a workable mechanism for shifting some of the economic burden of managing the program to the employer. For the above reasons it is recommended that policymakers encourage and assist organized labor in its interest in promoting alcoholism treatment for membership. A related recommendation is that some program of federal or state incentive or subsidy be developed to underwrite program costs until such a reimbursement mechanism can become routinized. EHP did not prove to be economically self-sufficient, simply because it did not have support during the interim between government funding and such a period of routinized insurance reimbursement.

In advocating the above approach to diffusing industrial alcoholism programs, it is realized that a major segment of the work force, that is, nonunionized and higher-level professional and managerial workers, might be excluded from the treatment population. While such groups have traditionally been virtually exempt from identification and referral from many company programs, this phenomenon has been considered by program sponsors and planners to be a flaw in existing identification procedures that can be corrected with time. While EHP had limited experience in dealing with this segment of the problem-drinking work force, it may well be that the time has come to consider studying alternatives to the traditional mechanisms for reaching higher-level problem drinkers. Moreover, even if traditional identification and referral systems were successful in getting more higher-level workers into treatment, the realities of different cultural views, life experiences, and attitudes toward drinking itself would probably dictate the need to evolve an entirely different set of treatment plans for higher-status, predominantly white employees than is appropriate for blue-collar, predominantly black workers.

In studying alternatives for reaching and treating higher-level workers, however, one important factor needs to be kept in mind. Although it has been widely accepted that employers apply cost-benefit determinations in their decisions to extend assistance to workers, this notion is based largely on untested assumptions. Indeed, the research of other investigators, as well as findings from the EHP population, suggest that higher-status workers, both within the blue-collar class as well as among professional and managerial workers, may have even less job security than lower-status workers when both are identified under company treatment programs. Not only is there the possibility of a greater tolerance of deviance among lower-status workers, but as regards professionals and managers, most of whom are outside the collective-bargaining structure, there is no grievance mechanism to protect the worker dismissed for "unacceptable behavior."

Related to the evolution of EHP as a facility servicing primarily blue-collar workers is the issue of "penetration." While the actual percentage of alcoholics or problem drinkers in any given work force has never been empirically determined, estimates range from 3 to 8 percent. However, EHP was able to "penetrate," that is, to give services, to less than 0.5 percent. Clearly, even if EHP's target population is defined as the blue-collar work force, only a fraction of all possible problem drinkers in the work force at risk were identified and referred. It is important to point out here, however, that funding for a full-scale penetration effort was never provided for or envisioned. The project was designed first as a vehicle for obtaining basic data on work roles of problem drinkers and for determining whether treatment could prolong their labor force participation, and second to test the feasibility of offering treatment via the multiparty approach.

In conclusion, the findings from EHP's three-year demonstration and research project suggest a number of areas for further research into the work-related aspects of problem drinking. As mentioned above, research is needed on methods to reach "harder-to-identify" professional and managerial problem drinkers. Also needed are more refined estimates of the prevalence of alcoholism and problem drinking in the work force, not only according to type of industry but also according to occupational status of workers. While it is recognized that barriers to generating accurate estimates are formidable, without more precise indicators of the actual prevalence of the problem that identification and treatment are meant to attack, the extent to which any intervention effort is successful in penetrating the problem can only be guessed.

With respect to the identification and referral process, findings from the EHP supervisors' interviews suggest a number of areas for further research. Primary among these is the extent to which supervisors are able to identify problem-drinking employees on the basis of poor job performance rather than on the basis of the visible signs of drinking, which do not manifest themselves until relatively late in the progress of the problem-drinking cycle. Also of interest would be further analysis of supervisors' attitudes toward the confrontation strategy. Interestingly, EHP supervisors expressed the belief that the approach to confrontation in which supervisors are barred from mentioning their suspicion of the worker's problem actually worked against getting patients to treatment as early as possible. Another area of needed research is the nature of the evoluion of the identification and referral mechanism under union-operated treatment programs for problem drinkers, and the role that management will play in referring workers to a treatment resource managed by organized labor.

Examination of the work force characteristics and attitudes of EHP study workers has opened a number of suggestions and hypotheses that will require validation in future research. While EHP workers did not express a greater degree of job dissatisfaction than nonproblem drinkers in the same work force, alcoholic workers did express much higher levels of overall life goal frustrations. Additional study, preferably with the use of unstructured, open-ended research instruments, will be required to better understand the apparent differential accommodation and acceptance of a lower status in society between alcoholic and nonalcoholic workers.

While preliminary findings on job retention and clinic experience of the EHP study population have suggested many individual as well as work organization characteristics of workers that may be related to treatment outcomes, there is a need for controlled, multifactorial analyses of treatment outcomes among working class employed problem drinkers. Also needed are longitudinal investigations to determine the extent of recidivism and labor force stability following treatment.

Appendix: The Intake Questionnaire

As mentioned in chapter 1, the primary scource of data on referred workers was the intake questionnaire which appears in this appendix. In addition to generating data that could be used to test concepts developed in previous research, the instrument was constructed to yield data similar in form to that previously developed and widely known to the research communities both in alcoholism and in manpower research. Thus, occupations were coded following the U.S. Census of Population Occupational Classification System (U.S. Bureau of the Census 1971), work satisfaction questions were constructed to resemble the most common and authoritative opinion research instruments (Robinson et al. 1969), and alcohol consumption questions were included identical to those used in the patient intake questionnaire of the National Institute on Alcohol Abuse and Alcoholism (Stanford Research Institute 1974). Additionally, a number of questions designed specifically for the purpose of the present research were included in the questionnaire.

The questionnaire was pretested during a "walk-through" of the clinic one month prior to opening by fifteen members of local Alcoholics Anonymous (AA) groups who voluntarily underwent the initial clinical routines and were interviewed, using a draft intake questionnaire. As a result of the pretest, the questions in the instrument were reordered and a number of them changed. The final draft was pretested, using another ten members of AA.

To assure maximum reliability, the questionnaire and interview were designed with structured and repeated questions, and many questions were interrelated to provide intraquestionnaire consistency checks. To further ensure similarity in data collection, a manual on interviewer instructions was prepared. Fortunately, the majority of questionnaires were administered by one, highly trained, former Census Bureau enumerator who worked for the project in the sole capacity of interviewer, and this has also served to minimize interviewer variance.

The validity of the questionnaire was more difficult to test, although several responses have been validated with information from employer-supplied work histories, and the interviewer verified certain responses with the patient's counselor after completing the interview. Moreover, the instrument contains many questions whose reliability and validity have already been demonstrated by other investigators. Additionally, a number of validity checks were built into the questionnaire and interviewing format. "Assumption" and "adverse" questions were included to break pattern sets and retard cliché answers. Respondents were encouraged to answer rapidly in order to elicit uniformity in recall, and the interviewer was instructed to use random probing to assure that the intent of the question was clear to the respondent.

117

Intake Questionnaire

Referral

1   Who referred you for treatment?

2a   How did you hear about the clinic?

2b   Why did you think it was appropriate for you to come to the clinic?

3a   What was the reason for your referral?

3b   Do you think the referral was appropriate?

3c   Explain.

4a   Do you see a need for treatment?

4b   Explain.

5   What do you want treatment to do for you?

6   What do you expect to happen in treatment?

7a   Do you think that the Employee Health Program (as described to you) will meet your needs?

7b   Explain.

Employment History

8a   For what company are you presently working?

8b   What department?

9a   How long have you been at your most recent job?

9b   How many job changes have you had within your present company?

9c   How many different supervisors have you had while with your present company?

10   What is your current occupation?

11a Did you ever have training (other than on-the-job training) for your current job?

11b Do you presently use this training on your current job?

11c Was this training paid for by the company?

11d Did you ever receive any on-the-job training?

12a In the last twelve months, how many weeks have you worked, either full time or part time?

12b When you worked, how many hours a week did you work on the average?

12c In the weeks when you were not working, were you looking for work?

12d What was the main reason for your not looking for work during the weeks you were not working or looking?

1. Did not want to work.
2. Ill or disabled.
3. In school.
4. Could not find work.
5. Only temporarily laid off.
6. Other, specify.
7. Disciplinary suspension.

13a Prior to your present employment, who was your last employer?

13b How long did you work for him?

13c At what job?

13d How many job changes did you have within the company?

13e How many different supervisors did you have while with that company?

13f What was your gross salary per year?

13g What was your reason for leaving?

14a During the last five years, for how many employers have you worked?

14b During the last five years, how many times have you been unemployed?

15   What was your father's occupation?

16   How old were you when you held your first job?

Income

17a   What was the gross income earned by you last month?

17b   What was the shared gross income of the household in which you lived last month?

17c   What was the approximate shared gross income of the household in which you lived last year?

17d   What was your major source of income last month?

17e   What was your second most important source of income last month?

17f   Do you presently hold more than one job?

Attitudes Toward Job

18a   What do you do in your job?

18b   What skills and abilities are essential to your job performance?

19   How many people do you supervise?

20a   How large is the department in which you work?

20b   With how many other persons do you work, specifically in the performance of your job?

20c   How many people depend on you in the successful performance of their jobs?

20d   On how many people do you depend in the performance of your job?

20e   How do you get along with the people with whom you work?
1. Like them a lot.
2. Comfortable with them.
3. They are O.K.
4. Do not like them.
5. Other, specify.

20f Are any of your coworkers friends whom you see outside of work?

21 Some jobs provide a great deal of opportunity to learn more about the work and enable a person to increase his knowledge of the process and his skill; other jobs provide few such opportunities to learn more. How is it on your job?

1. There are very great opportunities to learn more.
2. There are fairly good opportunities to learn—above average.
3. There is little opportunity to learn.
4. There is almost no opportunity on my job to learn more about the process or to increase my skill.

22 Different jobs and types of work vary in how much opportunity they provide a person to advance himself, to be promoted. How is your job?

1. On my job there is no real chance to get ahead.
2. There is some chance to get ahead, but very little.
3. The chances of getting ahead are above average.
4. On my job there are excellent chances of getting ahead, in comparison with other lines of work.

23 Does management where you work put emphasis on your doing quality work or do they emphasize other things such as quantity of output?

1. Management puts heavy emphasis on the quality of my work.
2. Management emphasizes the quality of my work more than they emphasize other things such as quantity.
3. Management puts equal emphasis on quality and other things such as quantity.
4. Management emphasizes other things such as quantity more than they do quality of my work.
5. Management puts almost all the emphasis on things other than the quality of my work.

24a Which statement best describes your job?

1. I have no freedom at all to do my work as I want.
2. I have little freedom to do my work as I want.
3. I am fairly free to do my work as I want.
4. I am completely free to do my work as I want.

24b Do you work on a specific time schedule or are your hours flexible?

24c What hours do you work.

1. Days.
2. Afternoons.
3. Nights.
4. Swing, rotating.

5. When wanted.
6. Wheather permitting.
7. Other.

24d   Do you have decision-making power in policies concerning your job?

24e   Explain.

24f   Which statement best describes your job?

1. Most of the time I know what is required of me.
2. Sometimes I do not know what is required of me.
3. Often I do not know what is required of me.
4. Most of the time I do not know what is required of me.

24g   Which of the following statements best describes your job?

1. My work is checked constantly.
2. My work is checked at the completion of each task.
3. My work is checked at certain fixed intervals.
4. My work is checked at varying intervals.
5. My work is rarely, if ever checked.

25a   Do you consider your job routine?

25b   Explain.

26   What other opportunities exist within your company for you job skills?

1. None.
2. One, some, or few.
3. Many.
4. Other.

27   What opportunities exist in the general job market for a person with your skills?

1. None.
2. One, some, or few.
3. Many.
4. Other.

28a   Is your job boring?

28b   Explain.

29a   Would you want your son/daughter to pursue this line of work?

29b Explain.

30a The job you have now, is it the best one you have ever had?

30b Do you think the job you have now is the best one you will ever have before you retire?

31 If you were completely free to go into any type of job you wanted, what would be your choice?

1. Same type of job you now have.
2. Retire, not work at all.
3. Some other job to the kind you now have.

32 How often have you thought very seriously about making a real effort to enter a new and different type of occupation?

1. Very often.
2. Once in a while.
3. Hardly ever.
4. Never.
5. Already did it.

33 Which of the following statements best tells how you feel about changing your job?

1. I would quit my job now if I had something else to do.
2. I would take almost any other job in which I could earn as much as I am earning now.
3. My job is as good as the average and I would just as soon have it as any other job, but would change jobs if I could make more money.
4. I am not eager to change jobs but would do so if I could make more money.
5. I do not want to change jobs even for more money because the one I have now is a good one.

34 How well would you say your job measures up to the kind you wanted when you first took it?

1. It is very much like the kind of job you wanted.
2. It is somewhat like the job you wanted.
3. It is not very much like the job you wanted.

35 How frequently does it bother you that there is little opportunity to learn more about your work?

1. Nearly all the time.
2. Very often.

3. Sometimes.
4. Rarely or never.
5. I have the opportunity to learn.

36 How frequently does it bother you that there is very little or no chance to get ahead on your job?

Same as 35.

37 How frequently does it bother you that management emphasizes other things more than the quality of your work?

Same as 35.

38 How frequently does it bother you that there is only little or no variety on your job?

Same as 35.

39 How frequently does it bother you that there is little or no freedom to do your work as you want to?

Same as 35.

40 Which of the following statements fits your job?

1. Almost any one could do my job.
2. A good many people could do my job.
3. Only a limited number of people could do my job.
4. Very few people could do my job.

41 Compared that what you had hoped for when you finished school, are you

1. Better off than you hoped for at that time.
2. Not as well off as you hoped for.
3. Just about as well off as you had hoped for.

42 Compared with where you were ten years ago, are you

1. Further ahead in the things you have wanted out of life.
2. Behind.
3. The same as where you were ten years ago.

43 Suppose people like yourself lost their jobs. Out of every 100 people like yourself in that situation, how many do you think would find a new job in about one month?

44 How much of the time are you satisfied with you job?

1. Most of the time.
2. A good deal of the time.
3. About half of the time.

4. Occasionally.
5. Hardly ever or never.

45a How satisfied would you say you are now with your pay, fringe benefits, and working conditions?

1. Very satisfied.
2. Somewhat satisfied.
3. Not satisfied.
4. Not at all satisfied.

45b How does this compare with your satisfaction three years ago?

1. More satisfied.
2. About the same.
3. Less satisfied.

46a How satisfied would you say you are now with your opportunity to do interesting and enjoyable work?

Same as 45a.

46b How does this compare with your satisfaction three years ago?

Same as 45b.

Sociodemographic Characteristics

47a Does your spouse work?

47b What is her occupation?

47c Does she work full time or part time?

47d Are you a member of a union?

47e To which union do you belong?

48   Birthdate.

49   State of birth.

50   Sex.

51   Ethnicity:

1. Black, U.S. Born.
2. Black, not U.S. born.
3. White, U.S. born.

4. White, not U.S. born.

5. Other, specify.

52a What religion was practiced in the home when you were growing up?

1. Protestant.
2. Catholic.
3. Jewish.
4. None.
5. Other, specify.

52b What religion do you practice currently?

Same as 52a.

53a Marital status—present:

1. Never married.
2. Married.
3. Widowed.
4. Divorced/annulled.
5. Separated.
6. Other, specify.

53b If separated, divorced, or widowed, how long has it been since you last lived with your spouse?

53c How many times have you been married?

53d How old were you the first time that you married?

54a Do you live alone or with others?

54b Including yourself, how many people live in your home?

54c How many children do you have in or out of the home?

54d How many dependents do you have in or out of the home? (This refers to persons dependent on you for 50 percent of their support.)

55a In how many different places (addresses) have you lived in the last five years?

55b How long have you lived in Maryland?

55c What is the zip code of your present address?

55d How long have you lived at your present address?

55e What type of residence do you live in?

    1. Room.
    2. Apartment.
    3. House, mobile home.
    4. Other, specify.

55f Do you rent or own your own home?

56a What is the highest grade you have completed in school?

56b In what year did you complete this grade?

56c If you have not completed high school, have you earned a high school equivalency or GED?

56d When did you get it?

Drinking Behavior and Treatment History

57a How would you generally say your health was during the last year?

    1. Excellent.
    2. Good.
    3. Fair.
    4. Poor.

57b Is your health right now better or worse than a year ago?

57c How many times have you seen a doctor during the last year?

57d How many times have you seen a dentist during the last year?

57e How many times have you been hospitalized during the past year?

57f How many times of these were alcohol-related?

57g During the last year how many times have you been to the outpatient clinic of a hospital?

57h How many of these times have been alcohol-related?

58a Do you drive a car, truck, or other motor vehicle?

58b How many traffic tickets have you received for drinking and driving during the past year?

58c   How many times have you been arrested for drinking, not related to driving during the past year?

58d   How many times have you been in jail for any reason?

58e   How many times have you driven under the influence of alcohol during the past year?

58f   Have you been sent to the Alcohol Safety Action Project (ASAP) during the past year?

59a   At approximately what age did you start drinking frequently or heavily? (More than three times a week.)

59b   Approximately how many years have you been drinking frequently or heavily?

60   Family drinking—fill out the following chart. Indicate whether any of the following people drank occasionally, frequently, or constantly when you were growing up. If the person listed was not in the home, code "not present." Code only *one* number per person.

60a   Did your father drink?

1. Not present.
2. No.
3. Occasionally.
4. Frequently.
5. Constantly.

60b   Did your mother drink?

Same as 60a.

60c   Did your brother or sister drink?

Same as 60a.

60d   Did any other person drink? If so, specify.

Same as 60a.

60e   Do you think any of the above persons had a drinking problem?

60f   If yes, specify who.

61   Household drinking—now I am interested in knowing about the drinking done by persons you are living with presently. Does anyone drink occasionally, frequently, or constantly? If the person listed does not live in your household, code "not present" for each person. Code only *one* number per person.

61a Does your spouse dinrk?

Same as 60a.

61b Do any of your children drink?

Same as 60a.

61c Does your father drink?

Same as 60a.

61d Does your mother drink?

Same as 60a.

61e Does your brother or sister drink?

Same as 60a.

61f Does any other person drink? If so, specify.

Same as 60a.

61g Do you think any of the above persons have a drinking problem?

61h If yes, specify who.

61i Are any of the individuals listed above presently receiving alcoholism treatment?

61j If yes, specify who.

62a How long has it been since you have had your last drink?

    1. 1–16 days.
    2. 17–29 days.
    3. 1–5 months.
    4. 6–11 months.
    5. 1–2 years.
    6. Over 2 years.

62b What has been your longest period *without* a drink during the last three months?

    1. None.
    2. 1–2 days.
    3. 3–6 days.
    4. 1–2 weeks.
    5. 3–4 weeks.
    6. 5–8 weeks.
    7. Over 2 months.

62c How many days have you had a drink during the last month?

62d How many days did your most recent drinking "bout" last?

63a During the past month have you had any beer?

63b How often did you drink beer?

1. Constantly.
2. Everyday.
3. Nearly everyday.
4. 3–4 days a week.
5. 1–2 days a week.
6. Weekends only.
7. Less than once a week.

63c About how much beer did you drink in a typical day?

1. 6 quarts or more.
2. 5 quarts.
3. 4 quarts.
4. 3 quarts.
5. 1–2 quarts.
6. 1–3 glasses.

64a During the past month, have you had any wine?

64b How often did you drink wine?

Same as 63b.

64c About how much wine did you drink on a typical day?

1. 5 fifths or more.
2. 3–4 fifths.
3. 2 fifths.
4. 1 fifth.
5. 2 or 3 waterglasses or 4–6 wine glasses.
6. 1 waterglass or 1 or 2 wine glasses.

65a Have you had any whiskey, gin, or other hard liquor during the past month?

65b How often did you drink any hard liquor?

Same as 63b.

65c How much hard liquor did you drink in a typical day?

1. 4 pints or more.
2. 3 pints.

3. 2 pints.
4. 1 pint.
5. 11–14 shots.
6. 7–10 shots.
7. 4–6 shots.
8. 1–3 shots.

66a When do you usually drink?

1. Weekends only.
2. Weekdays only.
3. Weekends and weekdays.

66b During weekends when do you usually drink and how much?
Evening

1. Beer (number of 12-oz. cans).
2. Wine (number of 6-oz. glasses).
3. Liquor (number of 1.5-oz. shots).

Afternoon

1. Beer.
2. Wine.
2. Liquor.

Morning

1. Beer.
2. Wine.
3. Liquor.

66c Do you usually drink alone or with others on weekends?

66d During the week, when do you usually drink and how much?
Same as 66b.

66e Do you usually drink alone or with others on weekdays?

66f Do you drink at work?

1. Regularly.
2. Frequently.
3. Occasionally.
4. Rarely.
5. Never.

66g When do you usually drink at work and how much do you drink?
Evening

1. Beer.

2. Wine.
3. Liquor.

Afternoon

1. Beer.
2. Wine.
3. Liquor.

Lunch

1. Beer.
2. Wine.
3. Liquor.

Morning

1. Beer.
2. Wine.
3. Liquor.

66h Why do you drink at work?

1. Relax—release—calm—nerves.
2. Boredom—nothing else to do.
3. Arrive drunk.
4. Others drinking.
5. Want it.
6. Other.

66i Do most of your friends drink?

1. Constantly.
2. Frequently.
3. Occasionally.
4. Never.

66j Do you think any of your friends have a drinking problem?

66k Do the people you work with drink?

Same as 66i.

66l Do you think any of the people you work with have a drinking problem?

67a How many times have you been drunk in the last month?

1. None.
2. 1–4.
3. 5–10.
4. More than 10.

67b What was the longest period you went between drinks in the last month?

1. 12 hours or more.
2. Less than 12 hours.

67c What was the longest period of continued drinking in the last month?

1. Less than 6 hours.
2. 6–12 hours.
3. More than 12 hours.

67d How many days did you have a drink upon awakening in the morning in the last month?

1. None.
2. 1–4.
3. 5–10.
4. More than 10.

67e How many meals have you missed because of drinking in the last month?

Same as 67d.

67f What portion of the time were you drinking alone?

1. Less than one-fourth.
2. One-fourth to one-half.
3. One-half to three-fourths.
4. More than three-fourths.

67g How many times have you had memory lapses or "black-outs" in the last month?

1. None.
2. 1–2.
3. 3–5.
4. More than 5.

67h How many times have you had the shakes in the last month?

Same as 67g.

67i How many nights have you had difficulty breathing in the last month?

Same as 67g.

67j How many quarrels have you had with other people while drinking in the last month?

Same as 67g.

67k Did you ever drink on the job or while performing daily activities?

1. Yes.
2. No.

671 How many days did you miss from work because of drinking in the last month?

Same as 67g.

68a How would you, yourself, describe your drinking at the present time; would you say

1. I don't drink.
2. I am a social drinker.
3. Sometimes I drink more than I should.
4. Frequently I drink more than I should.
5. I have a steady drinking problem.

68b Why do you drink?

1. Social.
2. Calms me down—relax.
3. Relieves pain (physical).
4. Boredom.
5. Like to—like taste—gives me pleasure.
6. Habit.
7. Loneliness.
8. Alcoholic.
9. Other.

68c At the moment, how serious a problem do you feel your drinking is?

1. It is no problem at all.
2. It is a slight problem.
3. It is a moderate problem.
4. It is a serious problem.
5. It is a very serious problem.

68d During the past month, would you say that your drinking problem

1. Has improved.
2. Stayed about the same.
3. Gotten worse.

68e What do you think you will be able to do in the next few months about your drinking? Do you intend to

1. Stop altogether.
2. Cut down.
3. Stay the same.
4. Drink more.

68f Do you worry about any of these things?

1. Getting and keeping a job you like?
2. Finding friends who don't drink?
3. Getting along with people?
4. Getting along with your family?
5. Finding a good place to live?
6. Your health?
7. Having enough money to live on?
8. Finding things to do in your spare time?

69 In the last month have you taken any drugs?

70a Which ones have you taken and how often have you taken them? (Asked for five different drugs.)

1. Antabuse.
2. Valium.
3. Librium.
4. Antipsychotics.
5. Respiratory remedies.
6. Gastrointestinal remedies.
7. Hypertension remedies.
8. Analgesics and antibiotics.
9. Other.

70b Number of days in the last month?

71a Have you ever been to an AA meeting?

71b Have you attended AA meetings during the last month?

1. Regularly.
2. Occasionally.
3. No.

71c Over a period of how many years have you attended AA?

71d Have you ever received any treatment for problem drinking other than AA during the last five years? (Asked for five episodes of treatment.)
Name of treatment

1. State hospital.
2. Residential treatment.
3. Outpatient.
4. Private physician.
5. Other.

Type of treatment

1. Inpatient.
2. Outpatient.
3. Medical
4. Other.

Number of days in treatment

Notes

Chapter 1
Background Goals, and Scope of the Study

1. Because many of the extensive questions on drinking behavior and life adjustment in the intake questionnaire (see appendix) were specifically designed to yield index scores that could be compared with scores obtained through a subsequent reapplication of the instrument (and hence to measure changes in drinking behavior), much data were obtained in the intake questionnaire that we were unable to use.

2. Epidemiological studies have, in fact, shown problem drinking to be more prevalent in the lower-social classes. This differential, however, probably accounts for only part of the exceptionally high proportions of low-status workers in industrial alcoholism treatment populations (Trice and Beyer 1977).

Chapter 2
History of the Program

1. The "broad-brush" approach argues that potential labeling and stigmatization are the most significant barriers to effectively getting alcoholism treatment to industrial populations; thus, any therapeutic efforts should be organized as part of a larger and presumably less threatening "troubled employees" effort which would deal with a host of problems presented by workers. The reverse position is that of programs designed to deal exclusively with alcoholic workers. The broad-brush versus exclusively alcoholism debate is discussed by Roman and Trice (1976).

Chapter 3
Identification and Referral

1. Although the project was not able to obtain employer compliance with the second commitment, as discussed in chapter 1, participating companies did, in general, fulfill their promise to retain workers who showed evidence of sincerely trying to rectify their performance, as will be seen in chapter 7.

2. For a discussion of the role of occupational program consultants in diffusing the concept of industrial alcoholism programs among companies, see U.S. Department of Health, Education and Welfare (1974 chapter 8).

3. The features of industrial alcoholism programs are discussed at length by Roman and Trice (1976).

Chapter 4
Treatment

1. For some illustrative criticisms of the disease model of alcoholism, see Cahalan (1970) and Trice and Roman (1972).

Chapter 5
Description of the Study Population

1. The categorization of occupations used in the EHP analysis was based on the U.S. Bureau of the Census occupational classification system (1970). Data on the Baltimore labor force are from the U.S. Bureau of the Census (1972).

2. Total consumption in Baltimore City is equivalent to that of the United States as a whole. The city's consumption budgets exceed those of the United States by 3 percent (Branch 1975).

Chapter 6
Comparison of EHP Study Workers and Their Non-problem-drinking Peers

1. As was noted in chapter 5, the EHP study population evinced a considerable amount of absenteeism in the year preceding intake, which surely resulted in some loss of wages. The income figures reported here, on the other hand, relate to normal wages or salaries, and at least in that respect, study and comparison workers proved to be very similar.

2. This discussion of occupational mobility considers four occupational status levels: unskilled occupations (laborers and service workers), semiskilled and skilled occupations (operatives and craftsmen), clerical workers, and professionals and managers.

3. For a review of the literature on etiological factors in work roles, see Archer (1977).

4. Many investigators of job satisfaction argue that simply asking respondents whether they are satisfied with their jobs produces artificially high estimates of worker content (Robinson 1969). Therefore, a second question, considered to be a more sensitive indicator of job satisfaction, was asked along with the more direct one.

5. Differences between the study and comparison populations were significant at the level of less than 0.005 on both questions.

Chapter 7
Job Retention and Clinic Attendance of the Study Population

1. It is important to note that these figures count as dropouts all patients who did not stay in treatment for at least one year, and thus include patients who dropped out of treatment after only a few visits as well as those who continued in treatment through the eleventh month.

References

AFL-CIO. *Labor-Management Newsletter*. Vol. 2, January-February 1973.

Archer, J. "Occupational Alcoholism: A Review of Issues and a Guide to the Literature." In C. Schramm (ed.), *Alcoholism and Its Treatment in Industry*. Baltimore: Johns Hopkins Press, 1977.

Baekeland, F.; Lundwall, L.; Kissin, B.; and Shanahan, T. "Correlates of Outcome in Disulfiram Treatment of Alcoholism." *Journal of Nervous and Mental Disorders* 153:1-9, 1971.

Bailey, M.B. "Alcoholism and Marriage: A Review of Research and Professional Literature." *Quarterly Journal of Studies on Alcohol* 22:81-97, 1961.

Belasco, J.A.; Trice, H.A.; and Ritzer, G. "Role of Unions in Industrial Alcoholism Programs." *Addictions* 16:13-30, 1969.

Blane, H.T.; Overton, W.F.; and Chafetz, M.E. "Social Factors in the Diagnosis of Alcoholism: I. Characteristics of the Patient." *Quarterly Journal of Studies on Alcohol* 24:640-663, 1963.

Branch, E.B. "Urban Family Budgets Updated to Autumn, 1974," *Monthly Labor Review* 98(6):42-48, June 1975.

Cahalan, D. *Problem Drinkers*. San Francisco: Jossey Bass, 1970.

Cahalan, D.; Cisin, I.H.; and Crossley, H.M. *American Drinking Practices: A National Study of Drinking Behavior and Attitudes*. New Brunswick,: Rutgers Center of Alcohol Studies, 1969.

Cahalan, D., and Room, R. *Problem Drinking among American Men*. New Brunswick, N.J.: Rutgers Center of Alcohol Studies, 1974.

Cline, S. *Alcohol and Drugs at Work*. Washington, D.C. Drug Abuse Council, 1976.

Clyne, R.M. "Detection and Rehabilitation of the Problem Drinker in Industry." *Journal of Occupational Medicine* 7:265-268, 1965.

Corder, B.F.; Corder, R.F.; and Laidlaw, N.D. "An Intensive Treatment Program for Alcoholics and Their Wives." *Quarterly Journal of Studies on Alcoholism* 33:144-1146, 1972.

Edwards, G.; Fisher, M.K.; Hawker, A.; and Hensman, C. "Clients of Alcoholism Information Centres." *British Medical Journal* 4:346-349, 1967.

Esser, P.H. "Conjoint Family Therapy with Alcoholics—A New Approach." *British Journal of Addictions* 64:275-286, 1970.

Franco, S.C. "A Company Program for Problem Drinking." *Journal of Occupational Medicine* 2:157-162, 1960.

Gerard, D., and Saenger, G. *Outpatient Treatment of Alcoholism: A Study of Outcome and Its Determinants*. Toronto: University of Toronto Press, 1966.

Gurin, G.; Veroff, J.; and Feld, S. *Americans View Their Mental Health*. New York: Basic Books, 1960.

Hallan, J.B. Health Insurance Coverage for Alcoholism Proposed Benefit Provisions (Washington, National Institute on Alcohol Abuse and Alcoholism, mimeographed, 1973).

Hardy, R.E., and Cull, J.G. "Vocational Satisfaction among Alcoholics." *Quarterly Journal of Studies on Alcohol* 32:180–182, 1971.

Harper, F.D. *Alcohol and Blacks: An Overview*. Alexandria, Va.: Douglass Publishers, 1976.

Hayghe, H. "Job Tenure of Workers, January, 1973." *Monthly Labor Review* 97:53, 1974.

Hochwald, H. "The Occupational Performance of Thirty Alcoholic Men." *Quarterly Journal of Studies on Alcohol* 12:612–620, 1951.

Kamner, M.E., and Dupong, W.G. "Alcohol Problems: Study by Industrial Medical Department." *New York State Journal of Medicine* 69:3105–3110, 1969.

Kissin, B.; Rosenblatt, S.; and Machover, S. "Prognostic Factors in Alcoholism." *Psychiatric Research Report of the American Psychiatric Association* 24:22–43, 1968.

Kornhauser, A.W. *Mental Health of the Industrial Worker: A Detroit Study*. New York: Wiley and Sons, Inc., 1965.

Kurland, A. "Maryland Alcoholics: Follow-up Study 1." *Psychiatric Research Reports of the American Psychiatric Association* 24:71–82, 1968.

Lipset, S.M.; and Bendix, R. *Social Mobility in Industrial Society*. Berkeley and Los Angeles: University of California Press, 1959.

Lundwall, L., and Baekeland, F. "Disulfiram Treatment of Alcoholism: A Review." *Journal of Nervous and Mental Disorders* 153:381–392, 1971.

McClelland, D.C.; Davis, W.N.; Kalin, R.; and Wanner, E. *The Drinking Man*. New York: Free Press, 1972.

Mandell, W. "Does the Type of Treatment Make a Difference?" Paper presented to the American Medical Society on Alcoholism, 1971.

Maxwell, M.A. "Early Identification of Problem Drinkers in Industry." *Quarterly Journal of Studies on Alcohol* 21:655–678, 1960.

——. "Alcoholics Anonymous: An Interpretation." Chapter 15, pp. 211–222, in D.J. Pittman (ed.), *Alcoholism*. New York: Harper & Row Publishers, 1967.

National Institute on Alcohol Abuse and Alcoholism. *Alcohol and Alcoholism: Problems, Programs and Progress*. Washington, D.C.: U.S. Government Printing Office, 1972.

O'Toole, J., et al. *Work in America*. Report of a Special Task Force to the Secretary of Health, Education and Welfare. Cambridge, Mass.: MIT Press, 1973.

Pattison, E.M. "A Critique of Alcoholism Treatment Concepts, with Special Reference to Abstinence." *Quarterly Journal of Studies on Alcohol* 27:49–71, 1966.

Perry, S.L.; Goldin, G.J.; Stotsky, B.A.; and Margolin, R.J. *The Rehabilitation of the Alcohol Dependent*. Lexington, Mass.: D.C. Heath and Company, 1970.

Plaut, T.F.A. *Alcohol Problems: A Report to the Nation by the Cooperative Commission on the Study of Alcoholism.* London, Oxford, New York: Oxford University Press, 1967.

Presnall, L.F. "Folklore and Facts about Employees with Alcoholism." *Journal of Occupational Medicine* 9:187-192, 1967.

Robinson, J.P. "Occupational Norms and Differences in Job Satisfaction: A Summary of Survey Research Evidence." Chapter 3, pp. 25-78, in J.P. Robinson, R. Athanasiou, and K.B. Head, *Measures of Occupational Attitudes and Occupational Characteristics.* Ann Arbor, Mich.: Institute for Social Research, University of Michigan, 1969.

Robinson, J.P.; Athanasiou, R.; and Head, K.B. *Measures of Occupational Attitudes and Occupational Characteristics.* Ann Arbor, Mich.: Institute for Social Research, University of Michigan, 1969.

Roman, P.M., and Trice, H.M. "Monitoring and Evaluation of Occupational Alcoholism Programming." In B. Kissin and H. Begleiter (eds.), *The Biology of Alcoholism*, vol. 4. New York: Plenum Press, 1976.

Schmidt, W.; Smart, R.G.; and Moss, M.K. *Social Class and the Treatment of Alcoholism.* Addition Research Foundation Monograph No. 7. Toronto: University of Toronto Press, 1970.

Schramm, C.J. "Development of Comprehensive Language on Alcoholism in Collective Bargaining Agreements." *Journal of Studies on Alcohol* 38(7), 1977.

Schramm, C.J., and DeFillippi, R.J. "Characteristics of Successful Alcoholism Treatment Programs for American Workers." *British Journal of Addiction to Alcohol and Other Drugs* 70:271-275, 1975.

Sheppard, H.L., and Herrick, N.Q. *Where Have All the Robots Gone? Worker Dissatisfaction in the '70s.* New York: Free Press, 1972.

Siassi, I.; Crocetti, G.; and Spiro, H.R. "Drinking Patterns and Alcoholism in a Blue-collar Population." *Quarterly Journal of Studies on Alcohol* 34:917-926, 1973.

Smart, R. "Employed Alcoholics Treated Voluntarily and under Constructive Coercion." *Quarterly Journal of Studies on Alcohol* 35:196-209, 1974.

Stanford Research Institute. *Industrial Alcoholism Monitoring System Development—Evaluation of the IAC Program.* Menlo Park, Calif.: Stanford Research Institute, 1974.

Sterne, M., and Pittman, D. "The Concept of Motivation: A Source of Institutional and Professional Blockage in the Treatment of Alcoholics." *Quarterly Journal of Studies on Alcoholism* 26:41-57, 1965.

_____ . *Drinking Patterns in the Ghetto, Volume I.* St. Louis: Social Science Institute, Washington University, 1972.

Straus, R., and Bacon, S.D. "Alcoholism and Social Stability. A Study of Occupational Integration of 2,023 Male Clinic Patients." *Quarterly Journal of Studies on Alcohol* 12: 231-260, 1951.

Strayer, R. "A Study of Employment Adjustment of 80 Male Alcoholics." *Quarterly Journal of Studies on Alcohol* 18:278–287, 1957.

Trice, H.M. *The Problem Drinker on the Job*. Ithaca: New York State School of Industrial and Labor Relations, Bulletin 40, 1959.

_____ . "The Job Behavior of Problem Drinkers." Chapter 28, pp. 493–510, in D.J. Pittman and C.R. Snyder (eds.), *Society, Culture and Drinking Patterns*. Carbondale and Edwardsville: Southern Illinois University Press, 1962.

_____ . "Alcoholic Employees. A Comparison of Psychotic, Neurotic, and 'Normal' Personnel." *Journal of Occupational Medicine* 7:94–99, 1965a.

_____ . "Reaction of Supervisors to Emotionally Disturbed Employees." *Journal of Occupational Medicine* 7:177–188, 1965b.

Trice, H.M., and Belasco, J.A. "The Alcoholic and His Steward: A Union Problem." *Journal of Occupational Medicine* 8:481–487, 1966.

_____ . "Supervisory Training about Alcoholics and Other Problem Employees." *Quarterly Journal of Studies on Alcohol* 29:382–398, 1968.

Trice, H.M., and Beyer, J. "Differential Adoption and Use of an Alcoholism Policy According to Skill Level of Employees." To appear in C. Schramm (ed.), *Alcoholism and Its Treatment in Industry*. Baltimore: Johns Hopkins Press, forthcoming.

Trice, H.; and Roman, P.M. *Spirits and Demons at Work*, Ithaca, N.Y.: New York State School of Industrial and Labor Relations, Cornell University, 1972.

Trice, H.; Roman, P.M.; and Belasco, J.A. "Selection for Treatment: A Predictive Evaluation of an Alcoholism Treatment Regimen." *International Journal of the Addictions* 4:303–317,1969.

U.S. Bureau of the Census. *Census of Population and Housing: 1970 Census Tracts*. Final Report PHC(1)-19 Baltimore Maryland, SMSA. Washington, D.C.: U.S. Government Printing Office, 1972.

_____ . *1970 Census of Population Alphabetical Index of Industries and Occupations*. Washington, D.C.: U.S. Government Printing Office, 1971.

U.S. Department of Health, Education and Welfare. First Special Report to the U.S. Congress on *Alcohol & Health*. DHEW Publication No. (HSM) 72-9099. Washington, D.C.: U.S. Government Printing Office, 1971.

_____ . Second Special Report to the U.S. Congress on *Alcohol & Health*. Rockville, Md.: National Institute on Alcohol Abuse and Alcoholism, 1974.

U.S. Department of Labor, "Dealing with the Problem Drinker." *Manpower*, pp. 2–7, December 1970.

_____ . *Job Satisfaction: Is There a Trend?* Manpower Research Monograph No. 30. Washington, D.C.: U.S. Government Printing Office, 1974.

von Wiegand, R.A. "Alcoholism in Industry (USA)." *British Journal of Addictions* 67:181–187, 1972.

_____ . "Lets Quit Kidding Ourselves about Our 'Good Programs'." *Labor-Management Alcoholism Newsletter*. Vol. 3, July-August 1973.

Vroom, V.H. *Work and Motivation*. New York: John Wiley and Sons, 1964.

Warkov, S.; Bacon, S.; and Hawkins, A. "Social Correlates of Industrial Problem Drinking." *Quarterly Journal of Studies on Alcohol* 26:58-71, 1965.

Winter, R.E. "One for the Plant." *Maryland Medical Journal* 19:97-99, 1970.

Index

Index

113. *See also* Liaison personnel;
Insurance reimbursement
United States Department of Labor,
xv, 2, 3, 15–16

Vocational training of EHP workers,
69–71
Voluntary vs. coerced referral, 64;
and treatment outcomes, 101–
104

White-collar problem-drinking workers.

See High-status problem drinking workers
Work environment, features of,
71
Work force stability of EHP workers,
74–75, 83–86
Work history of EHP workers, 83–86
Work performance, poor: as basis for
identification and referral to
treatment, 40–42; documentation of, 28, 40. *See also* Job
behavior of EHP workers

About the Authors

Carl J. Schramm is an economist on the faculty of the Johns Hopkins University School of Hygiene and Public Health. He has written extensively on the problems of work-related alcohol abuse and the economics of alcoholism treatment. During the 1976-1977 academic year, he was a Robert Wood Johnson Foundation Health Policy Fellow at the Institute of Medicine, The National Academy of Sciences.

Wallace Mandell is a university psychologist and professor of mental hygiene at the Johns Hopkins School of Hygiene and Public Health. He also serves as clinical director of the Comprehensive Alcoholism Program at the Johns Hopkins Hospital.

Janet Archer is a graduate student in the Department of Social Relations at The Johns Hopkins University. She has authored several articles on industrial alcoholism.